The Lost Coast of
Norfolk

The old Cromer jetty viewed across the East Beach, *c.* 1894.

The Lost Coast of
Norfolk

NEIL R. STOREY

The
History
Press

First published in 2006 by Sutton Publishing
Reprinted 2007

Reprinted in 2009 by
The History Press
The Mill, Brimscombe Port,
Stroud, Gloucestershire, GL5 2QG
www.thehistorypress.co.uk

British Library Cataloguing in Publication Data
A catalogue record for this book is available from the British Library.

ISBN 978-0-7509-4225-6

Half title page: East Runton fishermen, *c.* 1908.
Title page: Shannock fishermen, Sheringham, *c.* 1920. Left to right: 'Potter'
Hardingham, John 'Tar' Bishop, Elijah Farrow and 'Belcher' Johnson.

For
Christine and David

Typeset in 10.5/13pt Galliard
Typesetting and origination by
Sutton Publishing.
Printed and bound in England.

Contents

A cliff fall after severe storms at Cromer, 1912.

The Quay, Great Yarmouth, *c.* 1887.

Acknowledgements

Once again it has been a pleasure and a privilege to research and write a book about the county in which I was born, bred and still live, and which I so dearly love. In my travels I have renewed old acquaintances and made a good few more along the way. There are too many wonderful and generous people who have had a mardle with me and encouraged my work to name them all, but a few I must mention specifically, without whom this book would not have been so enriched: Peter Brooks, Peter Stibbons, Peter Cox, David Gurney of Norfolk Museums and Archaeology Service, Tony Mallion and the listeners of BBC Radio Norfolk, Michael Bean at Great Yarmouth Library, Alan Carr at Great Yarmouth Tourist Information, Charles Lewis, Ronnie Pestell, Tim Pestell, Veronica Sabin, Eric Reading, the late Henry 'Shrimp' Davies, Alan Hurn, John Nockells, Keith Skipper, Robin Limmer, Friends of the Norfolk Dialect (FOND), Jenny Brinkhurst at North Norfolk Railway, Dave King at the William Marriott Museum, Sheringham Museum, all my friends at Cromer Museum, Time & Tide Museum, Great Yarmouth, Clive Wilkins-Jones and all the staff at Norfolk Heritage Library, the Norfolk Records Office, University of East Anglia Library, Simon Fletcher, Clare Jackson, Michelle Tilling, Matilda Pearce and the wonderful graphics team at Sutton Publishing, my marvellous WEA students and the readers of *Norfolk Journal and East Anglian Life*.

Finally, and by no means least, I thank my family, especially my son Lawrence and partner Molly who have shared interest, research and travelled many pleasurable miles with me to the far-flung coastal corners of Norfolk as we researched this book.

All illustrations are taken by the author or from the author's collection, unless otherwise noted.

Two sturdy Shannocks. 'Belcher' Johnson and John 'Rook' Reynolds mending their crab pots, Sheringham, c. 1912.

Introduction

The Norfolk coast is a remarkable, beautiful and unique treasure in our sceptred isle. Over the years it has suffered and continues to endure constant coastal erosion and regular incursions by the sea. A number of towns, villages and hamlets such as Shipden, Keswick and Eccles have been lost beneath the waves or have been caused to move continually inland from their original foundation as the soft cliffs upon which they eventually found themselves perched were gradually eaten away by the indefatigable lap and crash of the waves. In this book I not only look at those settlements that have succumbed to or still struggle against erosion but also those that remain and have been changed irrevocably by the silting up of sea channels such as Castle Rising, the Burnhams and the Glaven ports, or have developed upon the sand bars created by longshore drift, where previously there was open sea such as Great Yarmouth.

The Norfolk coast is not only sculpted by natural forces, it has been shaped and is defined by its people, who have sought to embank, dredge and live from sea trade and fishing for centuries. Over the last 200 years there has also been the development of coastal resorts for health and holidays, initially only for the wealthy. The coming of the railways in the nineteenth century and the vast improvement of roads in the twentieth have changed the Norfolk coast beyond the comprehension of our forebears in a matter of a few generations. What were once tiny fishing villages, hamlets or open fields have become towns in their own right such as Hunstanton, Cromer or Sheringham. The old trades of boat building, coastal shipping and fishing have all changed, and their decline has impacted on the demographics of the entire coast.

I hope this book will be an enjoyable and nostalgic insight into the natural and man-made changes and development of the Norfolk coast along with their impact on its people. We will also encounter some of the personalities, folklore, events, disasters, heroes and villains that have become woven into the rich tapestry (or should that be fishing net) of its past. I also hope readers will be given pause for thought. Entire ways of life, trades, local character and communities that had survived for centuries have been lost, some now beyond living memory, some becoming increasingly remote or decimated. We should always remember with advantages, but perhaps we should all take the stories from these pages and consider the future and how much is still at risk of becoming part of the lost coast of Norfolk.

Low tide at the Millfleet near the sixteenth-century South Gate, King's Lynn, *c.* 1900.

CHAPTER 1

The Wash & King's Lynn

'Rising was a sea-port when Lynn was but a marsh, now
Lynn is the sea-port and Rising fares the warse.'
(Traditional Norfolk Rhyme)

As the county of Norfolk projects into the North Sea its promontory is further exaggerated by the great bowl of the vast wetlands known as the Wash. This unpredictable tract of coastline has the rivulets, creeks and channels carrying the waters of the Rivers Ouse, Nene, Welland and Witham snaking across it into the estuary. Its extent is some 17 miles long, 13 wide; it covers an area of 230 square miles and is bounded by Hunstanton's Gore Point on the Norfolk coast and Gibraltar Point at Wainfleet on the Lincolnshire Coast. About two-thirds of the flats here are dry at low water during spring tides and the remainder vary from 5 to 16 fathoms deep. There are virtually no fish in the Wash; this is mainly owing to the large breeding colony of seals. Therefore, the once numerous fishermen who navigated up the creeks harvested not shoals of shiny mackerel or herring but mostly shellfish, shrimps (particularly enjoyed by the late Queen Mother), cockles and mussels. At high tide their smacks would be anchored miles from land over the fishing grounds, where they would wait for the tide to go down. Once the waters departed and their boats 'landed' on what had been the sea bottom, they would jump overboard onto the drying sands and rake out their cockles or harvest the mussel beds.

The incoming tide of the Wash creeps up stealthily, covering all and rapidly turning narrow creeks into dangerous gorges and marshes into quagmires. Even those born and bred into working the waters here are ever conscious of the capricious dangers of this territory, which has been found out to the misfortune of many a weary traveller who thought he could effect a short cut to his journey across the marshes and flats. This was a journey most notoriously attempted by the baggage train of trappings and valuables belonging to King John, who after visiting King's Lynn in 1216 set out for Newark, Nottinghamshire via Wisbech, sending his chattels across the causeway over the Wash to arrive before him. Folklore tells of how the whole entourage was swept away by waves and engulfed by quicksands, never to be seen again. Treasure hunters are still searching for King John's treasure to this day!

A south-east view of Castle Rising by Nathaniel Buck, 1790.

The structure of the Wash has changed dramatically over the years. Rather than a case of coastal erosion eating away at the ports, coastal villages and towns, their waterways have become choked by the sediments swept into the vast mouth of the Wash by the North Sea and yet further clogged by the jet-black ooze collected by the rivers passing through the Fens. Such congestion has caused the shoreline to retreat, leaving coastal settlements and ports high and dry. One local rhyme recalls; 'Rising was a sea-port when Lynn was but a marsh, now Lynn is the sea-port and Rising fares the warse.' Known for its magnificent castle built by William d'Albini in 1138 there has been little archaeological evidence uncovered to support Rising as a great, flourishing port comparable with Lynn, but there was undoubtedly a trading staithe and market here from Norman times. The river channel is said to have been navigated by St Felix of Burgundy as far as Babbingly when he landed there in AD 630 and the first Christian chapel in Norfolk was erected near the site. The present church that stands there in tragic ruin was built to replace the earlier structure in the fourteenth century.

The low, swampy marshes between Rising and Babbingly, which often flooded in the spring tides (before the construction of the sea wall to the west), once carried this tidal river, capable of transporting trading ships, to a staithe near the village and even powered watermills at Rising. The Domesday Book records three mills, one fishery and a salt pan in Rising. This waterway would also have meant an easy method of transporting the Barnack stone for the facings of the castle and original church. By the Middle Ages Rising, and many settlements around the Wash, were ideally placed for the production of salt by the evaporation of seawater. Traces still exist of salt pans here, which were constructed at the high-water mark. The existence of an impressive stone market cross, also made of Barnack limestone, on the village green implies a Norman market foundation. A map of Rising Chase from 1588 shows a river passing between the lands of 'Rysinge and Babingley' to a watermill between the commons near 'Wharley Closse' and 'Goose More'. Small trading vessels were known to navigate as far as Rising staithe until about 1690 when the 'harbour' was closed by a sluice gate. There was once a continuation of the road leading north from the green of Castle Rising that descended to these marshes, bearing the ancient name of Haven-Gate or Havengate Lane. This was the area that Blomefield's *History and Antiquities of Norfolk* of 1805 notes as being 'very oozy', also recording a piece of an anchor that was dug up near here in the eighteenth century.

As the waters of the Wash receded people were not slow in taking advantage of this reclaimed land, grazing cattle on the marshes and harvesting the saltings of sea lavender and tasty samphire. The potential of man-made land reclamation was soon realised, and reached its height in the seventeenth century. The lands of the Duke of Bedford between Earith, Cambridgeshire and Salters Lode were drained according to the plans and methods of the Dutch engineer Vermuyden in 1637, which included the construction of the New Bedford river (the Hundred Foot Drain) and the first Denver sluice. Exactly 200 years later an extensive plan was drawn up for the reclamation of 150,000 acres of land from the Wash. This new land, planned to be about equal to the size of Rutland, was intended to be named in honour of the monarch – 'Victoria County'. The group of investors and engineers behind the scheme, which was estimated to cost £2 million, was headed by Lord William Bentinck and Sir William Ffolkes and included the eminent engineers

King's Lynn and its old wooden buttressed docks viewed from the west of the Great Ouse, *c.* 1900. The old creek in the foreground served West Lynn as a safe refuge for small boats and even trading vessels that ventured into its muddy contours.

Sir John Rennie and Robert Stephenson. The group, which became the Norfolk Estuary Company, was granted government approval for the project in 1848.

On 8 November 1850 work officially commenced on the drainage project to create Victoria County when the ceremony of turning the first sod was performed by Sir William Ffolkes, the Earl of Hardwick, the Earl of Leicester, Mr R.G. Tounley MP and Miss Wodehouse; each deposited a spade of earth upon a barrow, which was wheeled away by the Mayor of Lynn. A crowd estimated to number about 10,000 watched the ceremony. Work on the new drainage cut was progressing well until a dispute occurred between investors and the Wash ports opposed to the scheme, and a legal wrangle ensued. The result was financial strain and stress upon an already expensive project. The necessarily slow advancement of the work and the time and expense of getting the relevant Acts through parliament as it progressed killed the dream. Over the ensuing years only 4,000 acres of the Wash were reclaimed by the Norfolk Estuary Company and about 3,500 by others.

The fishing and farming town of Lin, Lenne or Leuna was known for trading and salt pans before the Norman Conquest, but it only really came to prominence when Bishop Herbert de Losinga founded St Margaret's Church in 1095 and the Bendictine Priory in 1100. From this foundation the town became described as Lynn Episcopai (Bishop's Lynn) and was granted its first Royal Charter by King John in 1204. The wealth of the town was further expressed at this time with the erection of chapels dedicated to St Nicholas and St James. Further religious houses were built in the town for Dominican, Franciscan, Augustine and Carmelite orders over the following 200 years. These were complemented by cells for lesser orders, by leper houses, hospitals, a host of almshouses, a pilgrim's chapel on Red Mount and finally the College of Secular Canons founded by Thomas Thoresby in 1500.

The Great Ouse which passed between Lynn and West Lynn in the eleventh century, then known as the Little Ouse, was said to be no more than 33yd across. During the reign of Henry III the monks of Ely made a new cut between Littleport Cahair and Rebeck, where it joined the main river and which took on the name of the Little Ouse, on the borders of Cambridgeshire, whence it now flows northward to the sea below Lynn. The resultant accumulation of water wore away and widened the banks of the river to help provide Lynn with a fine deep harbour and a waterway upwards of 300yd broad. Lynn's chief export from the twelfth century was corn, which was shipped to London and British coastal ports as well as Norway and the Baltic. By 1203 Lynn's foreign trade was such that the total duty collected was the fourth highest in any south- or east-coast port, including London. Further trade developed over the next 300 years, with Lynn importing a vast array of goods including German armour, wines from Gascony, wood and madder from Picardy, rarer Flemish and Italian cloths, and coals sailed in from Newcastle. Aristocratic requirements such as furs from Novgorod, gyrfalcons, hawks and lesser falcons from Iceland were also imported to the degree that in 1254 it is recorded that the King's tailor went to Lynn and purchased the equivalent of over £174 worth (a fortune in those days) of 'greywork' (the fur of the arctic squirrel taken in winter) from Edmund of Gothland.

The wealth of the port in 1374 is reflected in the fact that Lynn sent 19 ships, when Ipswich only provided 12 and Harwich 14, for Edward III's expedition to France. Edward also banned cloth imports and brought in the Flemish weavers who founded the great weaving industry in East Anglia that shaped and dominated the face of trade and wealth of this area until the Industrial Revolution some 400 years later. After the cloth import ban, exports of wool and cloth became one of the biggest exports from Lynn.

King Henry VIII granted Bishop's Lynn its first 'governing charter' in 1525 and constituted the burgesses of the town a 'body corporate' under a government of a mayor, twelve aldermen and eighteen common councilmen, with a recorder, town clerk and complementary offices. The King was no doubt aware of the dangers presented to the town from sea encroachments. Within his charter he granted the Corporation the right occasionally to tax the inhabitants for the construction and maintenance of defences 'against the violent raging of the waters hereafter happening'. After his dissolution of the monasteries Henry VIII claimed the properties and rights of the religious houses of Bishop's Lynn, granted a second charter in 1536 and, seeing the name of the town as rather incongruous, after his seizures changed the town's name to Lynn Regis (King's Lynn).

Lynn's magnificent Guildhall, c. 1910. Built for the Guild of Holy Trinity it was reconstructed after a fire in 1421, in the fine flint and freestone chequer-boarding seen here. Taken over by the Corporation in the sixteenth century, it served as a seat of civic government, administration and courthouse up to the twentieth century and is still used for civic purposes today. Those who faced the courts of Lynn did not have far to travel as the old Gaol House was only next door!

The Custom House on Purfleet Quay, King's Lynn, *c.* 1905. Built as a Merchants' Exchange in 1683 it was purchased by the Crown for a custom house in 1715.

By the fifteenth and sixteenth centuries the merchants of Lynn had become very wealthy. Their magnificent Guildhall was built for the Guild of Holy Trinity and rebuilt after a fire in 1421, in fine flint and freestone chequer-boarding. Taken over by the Corporation in the sixteenth century, it is used for civic purposes to this day. The larger Hall of the Guild of St George, now the arts centre, was also erected in the fifteenth century. The Lynn merchants also constructed themselves large and impressive houses near the market place and port, decorating and furnishing them in the style and under the artistic influence of their trading partners in Holland and their trading-partner ports of the Hanseatic League. Indeed, Lynn was so appealing that many tradesmen from the Low Countries emigrated and settled themselves there. A few fine examples of these buildings remain today around the quayside area near the Guildhall, and a magnificent range of fifteenth-century warehouses used by the merchants of the Hanseatic League may be found on St Margaret's Lane. Further south is the outstanding complex of Hampton Court, consisting of a merchant's house, counting house, warehouses and apprentices' quarters. By the late seventeenth century the aristocratic imports of furs and falcons had declined, but were amply replaced with expanded trade in stockfish (salted or dried cod) from Iceland (King Street was formerly known as Stockfish Row), wines and spirits from Spain, France and Germany, and wooden goods such as rafters and ship deal boards, masts, spars, pitch, resin and tar from the Baltic countries.

The Custom House on Purfleet Quay stands today as a silent memorial to the importance and value of sea trade to King's Lynn. Built in 1683 by Sir John Turner, a successful Lynn vintner who served Lynn three times as Mayor and for many years as the town's Member of Parliament. It was designed by his friend, Lynn architect Henry Bell (architect of a number of the town's buildings and a man who, himself, served two tenures as Mayor), and was originally intended as an exchange for merchants. The canny Sir John also had the fine Duke's Head Inn in the Tuesday Market erected in the same year for the use of visitors to his new Merchant's Exchange.

The Exchange was purchased by the Crown in 1715 for a Custom House to replace the old one in the Tuesday Market Place. The father of George Vancouver (1757–98), the man who acquired British Columbia for the nation, was a customs officer here. At that time eighty-five trading vessels (excluding fishing smacks), capable of handling a total tonnage of 12,700, belonged to the port, and there was boasted to be space for 200 sails to lie off its quays. No doubt inspired by the coming and going of the tall-masted traders George Vancouver went to sea at the age of 14, sailing with Captain James Cook to the South Seas. In 1766 he joined Cook on his ill-fated voyage on the *Discovery*, during which Cook was killed in Hawaii. Vancouver distinguished himself recovering his dead captain's body from the natives. As a captain in his own right Vancouver originally claimed Alaska for the Crown under the name of New Norfolk, but this would not last. He is, however, immortalised in the place name of Vancouver in British Columbia, and he introduced such local place names as Lynn, Point Snettisham and Holkham Bay to those foreign shores.

While Vermuyden's seventeenth-century drainages benefited the lands of the Duke of Bedford, the sluices at Denver and Salter's Lode caused the river navigation to Lynn to become impaired and the harbour to be obstructed with silt that was thrown up by the high spring tides. Lynn petitioned a complaint, and a survey was made by Colonel John Armstrong in 1724. The town's fears confirmed, Armstrong proposed that everything connected with the Great and Little Ouse rivers should be restored, as far as possible, to the state it was in before the execution of the new drainage scheme. Armstrong's report records the flood tide ran through Lynn Haven ordinarily for 3 hours and 4 minutes and that the common spring sides rose in height by 14ft; but, when propelled by a north-east wind, they sometimes flowed nearly 26ft perpendicular, forcing ships from their moorings and running over the quays into many of the streets and even into the Tuesday Market Place. The occasional tides that ran with unusual rapidity were known as the bore. These have been almost unknown since the Marsh and Vinegar Middle Cuts were made.

Sadly, the long delay enacting the improvements to the trading routes into Lynn caused an inevitable decline in its fortunes. By the early nineteenth century, the port described by Daniel Defoe in *A Tour Through the Whole Island of Great Britain* (1724–6), as 'a beautiful well built, and well situated town, at the mouth of the River Ouse . . . [where] there is the greatest extent of inland navigation here, of any port in England London excepted' was subject to the caustic rhyme:

> Ye rotten Borough of King's Lynn,
> Dead in trade, but alive in sin,
> Famous for unmarried daughters,
> Mud, and filthy tidal waters.

Lynn had maintained a whaling fleet since medieval times. Extant until the nineteenth century the fleet sailed every spring, equipped with harpoons, ropes, axes, rowboats and a motley assortment of some of the hardest men of the sea to hunt in the waters around Greenland. The whaler's return in August was greeted with the ringing of church bells and for weeks afterwards the town would reek of boiling blubber. One bumper catch was recorded in August 1818, when the whaler *Enterprise* arrived at South Lynn from Greenland under the command of Captain Sanderson. Eleven 'fish' were on board, which together would yield an estimated 160 tons of oil worth about £6,000, exclusive of whalebone and by-products.

Lynn's old mainstay exports were joined in the nineteenth century by trade in timber, linseed cake, the manufacture of artificial fertilisers from phosphates and potash imported from North Africa and Spain. It is worth recalling the men who went onto these hulks to unload manually the phosphates by spade into crane buckets that would then be lifted onto waiting wagons on the South Quay. Well into the twentieth century few of these men imagined the dangers they faced without gloves, with sleeves rolled up and flat caps on; the only protection they wore against the 'ash' dust were the scarves tied over their noses and mouths or the home-made masks fashioned from net curtains.

The old Fisher Fleet at Lynn's North End, *c*. 1908, crammed with scores of fishing vessels that once sailed out of this waterway to harvest shellfish, shrimps, cockles and mussels from the Wash. In the late nineteenth century 450 fishermen worked out of the port of Lynn in 140 fishing boats.

The river navigation was much improved in the early nineteenth century by diverting the stream from the old channel between Lynn and Wiggenhall St Germans bridge into a new channel called the Eau Brink Cut, which extends in a straight line for 2½ miles and is between 300 and 350ft wide, lessening the journey from Lynn to St Germans from 7 to 3½ miles. The Eau Brink Cut had been suggested by Armstrong in the 1720s but the costs involved meant there was no progress until 1795 when the first of eight Acts of Parliament were passed for the funding and construction of the cut. Progress was slow and work did not begin in earnest until 1818. It was finally completed in 1821, when on 31 July it was opened with due pageantry of decorated boats and thousands of spectators. The Eau Brink Commissioners borrowed the phenomenal sum of about £600,000 for the project. To pay back this debt and interest, and to maintain the cut, banks and bridges, the Commissioners were granted the right to levy a yearly drainage tax on the 320,000 acres of fens and marshes that benefited from the cut. The waterway was cleared and the channels improved to such a degree that 'two bottle-nosed whales' or 'finners' were captured a little below the harbour a few years after the cut was completed, and a 25-ton whale was caught in September 1842.

Between 1850 and 1853 another improvement scheme embanked the lower course of the Great Ouse into a canal and built long 'training walls' from the

The King's Lynn docks, *c.* 1900. At this time Lynn Docks attracted scores of tall-masted trading ships for the timber trade. Traders from Russia and Germany also brought in boatloads of linseed cake for cattle and then reloaded with coal, delivered to the docks by single-line railway, for their journey back.

harbour to stabilise the course of the estuary out into the Wash. In 1873 a new iron bridge replaced the old wooden crossing over the Ouse just above Lynn. Alexandra Dock was constructed between 1867 and 1869; joined by Bentinck Dock in 1883, the port was now able to host the new, larger steam-powered trading vessels whatever the vagaries of the tide; there was even a rail line down to the wharves. The construction of the new docks was no mean feat in its day. The navvies employed on Alexandra Dock excavated the 6¾-acre site to a depth of 31ft, equipped with just shovels, wheelbarrows and horse-drawn carts to haul the soil and sludge up the steep sides of the plot.

These new docks did not meet with approval from all quarters; protests were particularly vociferous from the Lynn fishermen. It was their ancient belief that the Fisher Fleet had been given to them in perpetuity by King John. From here the fishermen sailed in and out of port, and boatyards like Worfolk's, just south of the fleet, built their wooden boats by traditional methods. The construction of Bentinck Dock meant the Fisher Fleet was to be cut in half. When a boom was placed across the fleet the workmen and observing councillors had to be protected by policemen. The fishermen were overpowered by the law, both physically and on paper, but they would not go without one last gesture of defiance and they managed to pitch the Chief Constable's hat into the water and pelt the council men with mud. Today the fishing community which once spread along the North End of Lynn has long gone and, somewhat ironically, the area is covered with council houses.

CHAPTER 2

The Road to Hunstanton

This chapter not only travels the miles through some of the villages between King's Lynn and Hunstanton, but examines the metaphorical and historical road from the time when only open ground and sheep walks existed between Hun'ston lighthouse and Heacham to the creation of New Hunstanton a little over 150 years ago.

King's Lynn is situated on a great branch of tidal waterway where rivers and sea converge; strictly speaking, the first *coastal* trading settlements on our journey were situated at Snettisham and Heacham. No harbour could be constructed on the flat beach at Snettisham but trading vessels could get close enough in the deep waters just off the beach to land goods. This quiet, secluded beach was also popular with those who chose to flout the laws of customs and excise, and much contraband was landed here to endow the cellars of the local pubs, and to fill the tea caddies and the pipes of local folk. In one case recorded in January 1822 a smuggling boat landed eighty tubs of gin and brandy on the beach at Snettisham. The excise men were close by and seized the cargo, but a crowd of about 100 people, appearing out of the gloom armed with 'bludgeons and fowling pieces', assisted the smugglers in retrieving some of their confiscated goods and allowed them to make good an escape in their boat, while those on the beach made their getaway in the twenty or thirty horses and carts that were waiting on the beach to receive the contraband.

The Snettisham beach, which adjoins the Lynn channel, was endowed with an extensive bed of shingle that was dug out in immense quantities for a payment of 10*d* per ton to the Lord of the Manor. This shingle was taken in vessels to various destinations, but particularly to Lincolnshire, and used in the repair of roads. It is also in the parish of Snettisham that there have been quarries since the late tenth century for the distinctive bright golden-coloured carstone so typical of the houses built in this area, notably at Hunstanton, on the Sandringham Estate, and used by the Estuary Company for encasing the embankments of the Wash. The quarries were joined in the nineteenth and twentieth centuries by chalk pits and lime kilns. In the 1920s so large were the quantities of the shingle removed by the Snettisham Shingle Company that such work had to be stopped in the interests of coastal protection. Other pits were dug subsequently; they have now become flooded and form part of an RSPB Nature Reserve.

Queen Alexandra's bungalow, which once stood on the northern side of Snettisham Beach, *c.* 1915.

Snettisham Beach, *c.* 1928.

Hunstanton pier, c. 1910. Built between 1870 and 1871, the pier was some 800ft in length and 16ft wide. Joined by the first promenade in 1879 it was described as 'affording a spacious landing-place and an agreeable promenade . . . where the air is known to be strongly impregnated with ozone'. The majority of the pier was destroyed in a storm on 11 January 1978.

Despite such extensive digging, the shingle has been substantially replaced over the years as much of the material brought into the Wash by the North Sea is carried by the tides into Snettisham. (In August 1854 one of the largest items of flotsam washed up here was a whale 'of the beak species' some 29ft in length with a girth of 21ft. The record of this 'landing' concluded, 'When boiled, although the operation was unskilful, it produced 120 gallons of oil.') The tides build the shingle into a steep ridge on the edge of the marshes and coat the mudflats with hard sand to form a sturdy and level beach. Today more than a mile separates Snettisham's market place from its beach. In 1908 a bungalow was built on the northern side of the beach for Queen Alexandra, wife of King Edward VII. Built in a style to resemble similar houses in the Queen's homeland of Denmark, it included an upturned boat in an exterior wall that provided a comfy seat for four. In her sojourns at Snettisham Queen Alexandra was accompanied by her entourage of servants and occasionally visited by friends; but after her death in 1925 this charming cottage fell into disrepair and was eventually demolished. From the late 1920s onwards a 'second village' of holiday cottages and self-built bungalows was established on the seaward side of Snettisham. It was here that in January 1953 the sea tried to claim back its demesne during the east-coast floods. Many brave rescues were undertaken, but several lives were lost on that fateful night.

Heacham is a village that lives cheek by jowl with Snettisham and the sea. A small cell of Cluniac monks, known locally as Heacham Priory and subordinate to Lewes Abbey, was founded here in the eleventh century by William de Warrenne, 1st Earl of Surrey, who had been granted extensive tracts of land in Norfolk by William the Conqueror. Extant until the dissolution, this monastic property was granted to Thomas Howard, Duke of Norfolk, in 1537. Evidence of a market here can be traced back to 1272 and probably had even earlier origins. The sea here must have captured the imagination of young John Rolfe (1585–1622), whose family lived at Heacham Hall and in West Norfolk for many generations. After marrying in 1608 he and his by then pregnant wife boarded the *Sea Adventure*, one of nine ships bound for Virginia, for a new life as colonists. All did not go well. A fearful storm wrecked their ship and they were washed up on the Bermudas, where Rolfe's wife gave birth to a child which soon died. Undaunted, inventive crew members built two new cedar boats and the survivors eventually reached Jamestown, Virginia, in May 1610. The written accounts of this adventure soon reached England and it is probably upon this incident that William Shakespeare based his play *The Tempest*.

Rolfe and his fellow early settlers were beset with sickness as well as strife with the local Indian tribes. Despite the tragic deaths of both his child and later his wife, Rolfe distinguished himself as a fine local citizen and leader. He married the daughter of the most powerful Indian chief in the area, Princess Pocahontas, who in 1607 had saved the life of Captain John Smith by throwing herself between him and his potential murderers. Rolfe brought his princess bride and their child to England in 1616. She became an instant celebrity and was presented at Court. Sadly, the English climate did not agree with Pocahontas and, although preparations were made to return to her home territory, she died in March 1617 before her ship had even left the Thames. Rolfe married again and returned to Virginia, where he died in 1622. A fine alabaster bust of Pocahontas dressed in the typical English fashion of the day – tall hat, ruff and a fan of three feathers – was made by Otillea Wallace, a pupil of Rodin, and erected in Heacham Church in 1933.

Although there is no formal harbour here today, an area known as Heacham Harbour once existed between South Beach and Snettisham Beach where there was an outfall of the river. A recognised port in the Middle Ages, in 1301 Heacham was ordered to send ships to Berwick-upon-Tweed for the war against the Scots. During the medieval period and up to the sixteenth century ships could sail all the way to Heacham, and the harbour remained important enough for the Commissioners for Havens and Creeks to appoint Martin Cobbes, Thomas Charterys, Christopher Walpole and William Cooke as deputies in 1568. The tidal nature of the Heacham channel made it subject to sporadic flooding, especially during spring tides, when it became an increasing threat to life and property. A new outfall was created at Heacham South Beach, and all that now remains of the old channel is a silted-up creek. Parkin in his completion of Blomefield's *History of Norfolk* was in no doubt that 'the channel might be opened with great ease, and probably a century hence Heacham may be a town of great flourishing trade and commerce, and a dangerous rival to Lynn'. The 'harbour' was finally closed off in 1933; the watery channel is more silted and clogged than ever and Heacham remains a quiet village. William White described the village's situation in 1846 as 'sheltered behind a bold acclivity, at the foot of which a small rivulet flows across the salt marsh to the flat beach'. From the diversion of the channel up to the late nineteenth century coal

The once-navigable Heacham Channel and the old bridge, *c.* 1905. Behind the bridge to the left is Caley's Mill, now surrounded by the swaying purple fields of Norfolk Lavender Ltd.

vessels and sloops unloaded their cargoes on the sands of the beach, though only in summertime, riding at anchor here being unsafe in the wintertime. Local tradesmen would watch for the arrival of these trading vessels and send wagons down to the beach and shore ready to load from the boats.

The Domesday Book records three mills in Heacham; only one, built in the 1820s, remains today. Rendered obsolete in 1919 the mill was purchased by Ginger Dungate in 1935 in a semi-derelict state. Around this mill spread the fledgling business of Linn Childers and Ginger Dungate to grow and distil lavender. Their first harvest had been gathered in 1933 amid much media interest. The fragrant sacks of flowers were then taken by horse and cart to Heacham station and then by train to Long Melford for extraction of the oil. In 1936 they acquired three French copper stills so they could produce their own lavender oil and installed them on Ginger's farm at Fring. By 1941 their fields of lavender were also being grown on Sandringham Estate land, and so successful was their business that they incorporated Norfolk Lavender Ltd. The old mill was modestly restored in 1954 to allow it to be used for packing and storage. Further extensions and restorations in the 1980s saw the old mill become the centre of production. Today the swaying fields of lavender and the wonderful array of products made by Norfolk Lavender draw visitors and orders from all over the world.

Hunstanton has always been noted for two natural features above all others. The resort is the only one on the east coast to face west, with the result that many visitors are taken aback to see the sun apparently set over the sea rather than the land. The other notable natural feature is the cliffs, unique among those of Norfolk which are often low marram hills or tall clay and sand mixtures so easily eroded by the sea; here they are very solid, made up of three layers of rock known as white chalk, hard

Hunstanton cliffs looking towards Old Hunstanton, *c.* 1935.

red clunch and iron-brown carstone, embedded with dirty yellow-coloured stones at the base. These cliffs represent some of the sturdiest geology in Norfolk. It was, however, noted in 1890 that since 1853 21ft of cliff had been eaten away from in front of the lighthouse, though it must be remembered that this time span did include the biggest recorded fall of the cliffs here, which occurred in 1868 when an estimated 2,000 tons of rock fell from the cliff near the lighthouse.

The oldest structure left in Hunstanton is the ruinous chapel of St Edmund built in 1272 by the monks of Bury St Edmunds in honour of their martyr saint. Local legend has it that Edmund, the East Anglo-Saxon king of East Anglia, landed on the beach near here in AD 855 having sailed from Saxony to claim his kingdom. Another tale goes further in stating that he even spent the next two years here after his landing learning psalms. The chapel was used for about 400 years until it was left to fall into neglect. All four walls of the ruin stood until the nineteenth century, but tourists came and took small souvenirs and eventually the walls collapsed, leaving only a very meagre and heavily restored arch which still stands today.

By the time Roland le Strange, the first of the noble family to arrive in the county from Brittany, married Matilda le Brun, the daughter and heiress of a local Saxon chieftain, in about 1100, any significant settlement in the area known today as New Hunstanton was long forgotten. The principal land possessions of the le Strange family were in Shropshire; their Norfolk hall was built near the source of the River Hun. Thus the 'modern' settlement of Hunstanton was begun by Sir Roger le Strange in about 1310. Sir Nicholas added to the hall in 1578 and one of his great-grandsons, Sir Hamon, finished the northern portion of the great house in 1623 and completed the eastern portion south of the gatehouse and the south wing by 1626.

The hall was further restored and enlarged by Henry le Strange Styleman le Strange in a major work completed in 1836, but tragedy struck in 1853, when after catching fire the whole of the hall from the library and south dining room to the prayer room was reduced to a mass of smoking ruins.

Fortunately, the rooms of the hall were quickly cleared of paintings and furniture before the fire reached them and great efforts to save the north and east side were made by the breaking down of communicating portions of the building adjoining these sides. The damage was estimated at £10,000 but undaunted the family enlarged the north-east block and in 1873 the Victorian wing was built, partly over the site of the Elizabethan range destroyed by the fire. The hall remained in the hands of the le Strange family until 1948, when heavy taxation forced them to sell it. A Lancashire stockbroker acquired the property and converted it into flats before a second great fire raged through it in 1951. The le Strange family still exist today, and among their hereditary titles is that of Lord High Admiral of the Wash, which gave them rights to the north-west Norfolk foreshore 'for as far as a man could ride out to sea at low tide and throw a javelin'. Local legend tells of when Mercedes Gleitz, the cross-channel swimmer, set foot on the Hunstanton sands in 1929 after becoming the first person to swim across the Wash, and was greeted by the squire with the words, 'You do understand, madam, that everything washed up on this beach belongs to me?'

The few houses that huddle around the Church of St Mary the Virgin and the Neptune pub are just about all that remain of the old village of Hunstanton. This area was a well-known haunt of excise dodgers – indeed it seems they even had their own 'gap', as the wagon runs to the sea here are named Coal Gap, Cart

The ruins of St Edmund's Chapel and the lighthouse, Hunstanton, 1930s. When the lighthouse closed in 1921 its light was removed and the building was converted into a café. In the 1960s the lighthouse was restored to its original condition and is now a holiday residence.

Mercedes Gleitz when she swam the Wash in 1929.

Gap and Smugglers' Gap. In the churchyard can be found the silent testimony to this vicious past in the form of headstones of those attempting to uphold the laws against smuggling; namely William Webb of the Light Dragoons and 'the mangled remains of poor William Green. An Honest Officer of Government who in the faithful discharge of his duty was inhumanly murdered by a gang of smugglers in this parish'. Both of these men were killed in a fracas on 27 September 1784. Matters had not improved by 9 December 1835 when it was recorded that the schooner *Harriet*, on her passage from St Petersburg to Liverpool, was lost with her crew of eight hands off Hunstanton. The article continued, 'The wreckage washed ashore was immediately broken up, and part of it converted to private purposes. It is shocking to contemplate the lawless scrambling of the wreckers of this coast to obtain possession of the prey, in which they appear to be encouraged by the conduct of persons whose especial duty it is to prevent rather than encourage the abominable plunder here carried on.'

The story of the *Harriet* is a tragic one because Hunstanton also had a noble tradition of lifesaving and alerting seamen to the dangers of its coast. A lifeboat stationed at Hunstanton had been placed there as early as 1824 under the auspices of the Norfolk Shipwreck Association, but had been closed in 1843 leaving only the coastguard boat there as a possible rescue vessel. Local people petitioned for a lifeboat in the 1860s and sanction was given by the RNLI in 1867. The first and the next two boats which served here between 1867 and 1931 were all presented to the station by the Licensed Victuallers of England, and all proudly bore the name *Licensed Victualler*. The first two boats alone saved over 100 lives before 1900.

Warning lights for mariners were exhibited from the chapel at St Edmund's Point from early times, and became so ensconced in the psyche they were known as the 'Chapel Lights' long after the chapel had fallen into decay. The first formal lighthouse was proposed in 1663 in a petition to King Charles II by a group of prominent Lynn businessmen. Reliant on safe coastal trade, it was in their interests for a light to be established at the mouth of the Wash. In June 1665 King Charles issued the patent authorising the setting up of a lighthouse in the Chapel Lands on Hunstanton Cliff. This was a wise siting, as it is here at St Edmund's Point that the land rises to the highest point in the area, some 65ft, marking the termination of Norfolk's west coast and the calm 'bowl' of the Wash, and the North Sea proper begins. The grant of rights for the light was, however, not given to the businessmen but to the King's personal surgeon, John Knight of London, the financial benefits being a token of thanks to the royal physician.

In 1666 two towers were erected on the cliffs with blazing beacons at their summits to shine out across the Wash. When brought into line by eye the lights would guide seamen safely into the Lynn Deeps. One night in 1776 the light was abnormally bright as the entire station burned to the ground. The new light was rebuilt by Edward Everard under the direction of Ezekiel Walker. He installed the very latest means of illumination at his disposal – eighteen oil lamps with silver-plated reflectors. The new Chapel Light was boasted about in contemporary accounts as being visible for 7 leagues, or 21 miles, out to sea. In 1838 the Chapel Light was bought out by Trinity House. By that time it had the distinction of being the last operational lighthouse in private hands. The old light was soon demolished and a new one erected in its stead with two keepers' dwellings and an oil store

The Hunstanton lifeboat, *Licensed Victualler*, which served between 1900 and 1931, shortly after its arrival at the station. John Colman Riches, the Coxswain of the boat between 1902 and 1931, served a total of forty-five years in the lifeboat service.

Hunstanton lighthouse, *c* 1910.

attached. In 1863 a new light with a prismatic lens was added. In the early 1880s the light was altered from a stationary light to an occulting light 'which is eclipsed for two seconds in quick succession twice every half minute'. Shining from atop the 50ft tower the light could be seen up to 16 miles out to sea on a clear night (probably a more accurate measure than the 21 miles claimed of its predecessor). The beam cast right across the Wash, except to the west, 'where it throws a red glare on a dangerous sand bank 8 miles off called the "Roaring Middle" on reaching which vessels are expected to anchor until daylight'.

During the First World War the structures around the lighthouse were joined on the seaward side by a small wooden hut. Its purpose was kept secret. After the war it was revealed to have been occupied by Commander R.J.B. Hippisley RN. He was an early pioneer of wireless telegraphy, and it was hoped he might be able to intercept German radio signals directing the movements of their fleet and their Zeppelin raiders. Hunstanton was the first of a chain of listening posts along the coast and the little wooden building was known for years after as 'Hippisley Hut'. By 1920 the role of Hunstanton Lighthouse had been taken over by a lightship. Decommissioned, the lamp was taken down in 1921 and the property was put up for auction; it became a café. It was commandeered by the military in the Second World War as an observation post and gunnery control. Reverting for a brief time in the postwar years to a café the old lighthouse was sold again in 1964. Owned at the time by the local council their advert in *The Times* attracted seventy offers in two days and the lighthouse eventually sold for £4,740. Sold again in 1996 it has been beautifully restored, and can now be hired as an unusual holiday home blessed with some of the finest sunset views in the country.

In the early nineteenth century Henry le Strange Styleman le Strange would regularly take his morning constitutional with his friend Charles Bagot, strolling across the unenclosed sheep walk from the lighthouse across the 'New Park' and down to the sea to bathe before breakfast. Often they would not encounter another human being and the view between the lighthouse and Heacham was unobstructed bar a tiny smattering of isolated cottages. No doubt he stood at the foot of the sweeping green, where the vision of a New Hunstanton, or 'Hunstanton St Edmund's', played out many times in his creative mind. Here he visualised a triangle of land opening out towards the sea with houses, hotels and shops gathered around it.

The first structure built towards realising le Strange's vision was the Golden Lion Hotel, originally named the New Inn. Constructed in 1846/7 the inn stood in the middle of a meadow and quite alone excepting a couple of old cottages in the vicinity. Those who did not share le Strange's dream were soon pouring scorn on the whole project, calling the inn 'le Strange's Folly'. But he knew his foundations were firm and he marked the town's establishment by erecting the old village market cross of Snettisham (which his ancestors had removed to Hunstanton when they inherited the title and estates) prominently on the green of New Hunstanton. In 1859 the only roads here were a track to the Golden Lion Hotel and the Chingle Pit Road, now known as Westlegate. A coach ran from the Globe at Lynn to the Le Strange Arms at Old Hunstan. Horses were changed at the Dun Cow at Dersingham and a third horse met the coach at the bottom of Redgate Hill to help the coach up the incline.

A branch of the railway was opened at Hunstanton in 1862, and no doubt Henry le Strange could see his dream becoming a reality as the hotels and smart apartmented guesthouses began to spring up in the village. Perhaps this final realisation was too much for the great man, for he neglected his health in favour of

The Green, New Hunstanton, *c.* 1900.

New Hunstanton High Street, *c.* 1903. All construction and designs in New Hunstanton were controlled by Hamon le Strange who tried to be faithful to his father's vision.

work on his vision and died of heart disease the same year. The dream was not lost, however, as Henry's son Hamon employed architect William Butterfield to formally lay out the town.

Soon bathing machines appeared on the beach and, in keeping with the best holiday resorts of the time, such as Southend, Brighton and Bournemouth, a pier was constructed (1870/1) for a company of local investors with capital of £2,000. Works were conducted under one of the foremost pier engineers of the time, Mr J.W. Wilson, the man behind the piers at Bognor, Teignmouth and Westward Ho! Hunstanton pier was supported on cast-iron columns built on screw piles, and extended some 800ft in length and 16ft wide. Joined by the first promenade in 1879 it was described as 'affording a spacious landing-place and an agreeable promenade . . . where the air is known to be strongly impregnated with ozone'.

In 1872 the good air and waters had been recognised by the Venerable William Emery, Archdeacon of Ely, who saw to it that a convalescent home was established in two rented houses under the patronage of the Prince of Wales. The purpose-built Hunstanton Convalesent Home was designed as a memorial of thanksgiving for the convalescence of the Prince of Wales in 1872. Its foundation stone was laid by the Countess of Leicester in August 1877 and it was formally opened on Easter Monday 1879 by the Prince and Princess of Wales. Accommodating a total of sixty patients, the home cost £7,000 to build and was supported by voluntary subscriptions and contributions from patients. A purpose-built children's section of the home was opened in 1890.

In 1886 the present High Street was a small byroad with cottages on the east side and a piece of land used as a kitchen garden by Tamworth House to the west. This was only leased as open land but was eventually sold to Messrs George and Frederick Cole for £250. They sold it to Charles Mitchell who learned there was a growing need for the post office to be more centrally located – he offered the land to the government for the development, and so began the construction of New Hunstanton's High Street as it appears today. New Hunstanton was always intended as a holiday destination for well-to-do gentlefolk and nothing was built in the town without the stamp of approval of the le Strange family. All construction and designs were controlled by Hamon le Strange, who sought to keep the town in line with the vision of his father. Everything had to be of complementary style and primary building materials were to be carstone from the Snettisham quarries with Bath-stone dressings.

The *Guide* of 1873 stated, 'The new town of St Edmunds is in the vicinity of the railway station. Handsome and substantially built with the Royal (Golden Lion) forming the nucleus. The workmanship is careful and there are several classes of house. It is a block plan with the houses placed singly or in groups in masses

The recuperative value of good clean seaside air is well evinced by the purpose-built Hunstanton Convalescent Home; designed as a memorial of thanksgiving for the convalescence of the Prince of Wales in 1872, it was formally opened on Easter Monday 1879 by the Prince and Princess of Wales. Built to accommodate a total of sixty patients, the building cost £7,000 and was supported by voluntary subscriptions and contributions from patients.

The Sandringham Hotel, *c.* 1908, once the premier place to stay in New Hunstanton and conveniently situated near the railway station. Neither the railway nor the hotel is in existence today.

of irregular form and size interspersed with gardens and open spaces to avoid uniformity. There is an enforced similarity of style and houses for all "from the peer to the peasant". However the supply fails to keep pace with the demand.'

New Hunstanton was formally recognised and became a town under the Local Government Act of 1894, when it became a separate parish with its own Urban District Council. The foundation stone of the town hall was laid by Mrs le Strange on 24 February 1896, and the developments around the central green were finally concluded with the completion of this town hall, opened in the same year, by the Countess of Cottenham.

Well-turned-out day trippers in horse-drawn carriages and holidaymakers of the genteel classes arrived in their hundreds by train in the summertime and popularised New Hunstanton. They could stay at a host of quality guesthouses, private hotels, apartments or the huge Sandringham Hotel that once dominated the seafront and was situated at the head of the Great Eastern Railway link to the town. One of the most popular trips on the paddle steamers of the Skegness Steamboat Company was the run across the Wash to Hunstanton. By 1883 the paddle steamer *May*, one of the biggest on the east coast, was regularly steaming across filled to her capacity of 255 passengers. Leaving Skegness at 8.30 a.m. she would arrive at Hun'ston at 11 a.m. Most of the passengers then took the opportunity to visit the Norfolk residence of the royal family at Sandringham. Some took the train to Wolferton, while others hired one of the horse-drawn carriages that lined up along the road in front of the piers for the 8-mile drive. The return steamer journey got travellers back to Skegness for 8 p.m. The cost for the steamer journey was 3s.

From the late nineteenth century up to the outbreak of the First World War the popularity of Hunstanton was at its height. The town was subtly decorated with the colours and attractions of a seaside resort enjoyed by the middle classes. The pier was finally crowned in 1912 when the Mikado Concert Hall was erected at its head, and live shows commenced for the entertainment of visitors. Concert parties performed for at least twelve weeks in the season from an amphitheatre with a stage scooped out in a hollow in the cliff just north of the pier, and another live show was offered in an annexe hall between the Sandringham Hotel and the railway station, while the Town Hall Theatre offered a selection of plays. At the back of the parade were swings – some with boats, others with highly decorated wooden horses – and a few penny slot machines. A popular pastime for older children was to buy long poles or staffs sold by the seaside shops. These would be carried down to the sands and used to vault from rock to rock on the beach.

After the First World War the Revd Alfred A. Toms MA organised a fragrant garden to be laid out around the ruined chapel of St Edmund in memory of the local fallen. Despite the construction of a more modern promenade and an open-air bathing pool near the Sandringham Hotel in 1928, Hunstanton maintained its air of a genteel seaside resort until after the Second World War, when the suburban development of the town began. The holiday houses and bungalows in the area of South Beach Road became the first homes for families just starting out. Many of these young families were marriages between local girls and American

Children among the rock pools on Hunstanton Beach, c. 1905. A number of them are holding their long vaulting poles or staffs.

servicemen from the nearby airbases. When the horrific east-coast floods smashed over the promenades in January 1953 it was this little community that bore the brunt of the wall of water. Despite the brave rescues enacted by a number of local people and, notably, USAAF serviceman Staff Sergeant Freeman A. Kilpatrick and Airman 3rd Class Reis Leming (both of whom were awarded the George Medal), thirty-one people perished here on that fateful night. A memorial bearing the names of the victims of the 1953 floods at Hunstanton has been erected in the Esplanade Gardens.

Times were changing and the genteel pre-war world was fading fast, never to be revived after the Second World War. The bathing pool and Sandringham Hotel were demolished to make way for caravan sites and car parks, and even the rail link, which had hung on resolutely through the Beeching cuts, was finally closed in 1969. The pier had suffered fires in the 1930s and the pavilion was not rebuilt. A comedy film entitled *Barnacle Bill* was shot on the pier in the 1950s. The story told of how the new owner of a dilapidated Victorian pier in the fictional resort of Sandcastle was faced with hostility from local councillors, all of whom had vested interests in its demolition. To save the pier her owner breached it at the landward end and registered it as a cruise ship, *Arabella*, and thus the pier became a luxury liner that never left the beach. The real Hunstanton Pier was not so fortunate. It became a popular roller-skating centre and even had a zoo and a miniature railway. But, falling into decline and dilapidation, the majority of the pier was destroyed during a heavy storm on the night of 11 January 1978. No trace of it remains today.

Hunstanton water gardens, *c.* 1937. As sea walls were extended along Hunstanton's sea front in major projects between 1924 and 1932, promenades, ornamental gardens, a swimming pool, shelters and this boating lake were all created for the entertainment of holidaymakers. Little remains today to hint at their existence.

CHAPTER 3

Brancaster Bay & the Burnhams

Brancaster Bay and its adjoining settlements have some of the most significant archaeological remains to be found along the Norfolk coast. In prehistory a forest stretched from Brancaster Bay, beyond Titchwell, Holme and Hunstanton and into the Wash before snaking along the Lincolnshire coast between Skegness and Grimsby. Good scours by the sea frequently reveal evidence of tree stumps known to local folk of old as 'sleepers'. Archaeological examinations of the area recorded as far back as 1831 have revealed horns and bones evincing herds of deer and oxen inhabiting the region. The 1831 expedition also uncovered some evidence here of early man, notably a flint axe lodged in the remains of a tree in the peatbed. Without doubt the most outstanding find here in recent years was the Bronze Age timber circle at Holme-next-the-Sea, exposed by a sea scour and dubbed Seahenge. In 1998 fieldwork on the ring was begun by Norfolk Archaeological Unit. It was found to consist of fifty-five close-set oak timbers with an upturned 'stump' chair or 'altar' in the centre. The timbers were removed for preservation and analysis amid much public debate. They have been dated to about 2000 BC, but the reason for the construction of Seahenge, how it was built and who built it will no doubt remain a subject of lively debate for years to come.

The bowl of Brancaster Bay is shaped to the west by St Edmund's Point, named after the saint said to have landed at nearby Hunstanton in AD 855. Brancaster Bay terminates at Scolt Head, and the channel through Burnham Overy comes from Holkham Bay. Immediately below St Edmund's Point is the village of Holme-next-the-Sea. Here was the terminus of the Roman road known as the Peddar's Way, which comes up from Suffolk and traverses Norfolk from Brettenham to Holme. The road is constructed in the straight line that the Romans were so famed for, with its only bend at Hockham. There is no clear evidence for the reason why the road terminates at Holme but one compelling suggestion is that at this well-judged point the mouth of the Wash is closest to Lincolnshire; if there had been a ferry crossing this would have been an eminently suitable place for it, so that it could join up with a similar Roman road that came down to the sea near Skegness. Without a crossing here the long route around the bowl of the Wash combined with the flooded Fenland around it would have meant a journey of weeks from Norfolk to Lincolnshire for the Roman legions, as opposed to a couple of days sailing across on a ferry.

A view across the water to The Hard and West Creek at Burnham Overy Staithe, *c.* 1925.

Just a few miles along the road evidence can be found of undoubted Roman origin and purpose, for here was the Roman coastal fort of Branodunum. Constructed on an area known today as Rack Hill, archaeology has revealed that the fort was built in the form of a square from imported sandstone, enclosing an area of about 6 acres and surrounded by a defensive ditch. Aerial photography has revealed evidence of a headquarters building within the fort and the suggestion of at least one earlier fort on the site. Aerial images have also revealed the network of roads and buildings of a civilian settlement outside the fortification to the east and west that suggests a far larger and denser population of this area (about 2,000–4,000 people) than today. The fort is thought to have been the most northerly in a chain of about ten such strongholds built in the third century AD along the east coast and around to Portchester near Portsmouth as a defence against Saxon raiders attacking from the North Sea. Its purpose was to act as a base for Roman military units as they patrolled the coastline. Today there is no physical evidence for the existence of the fort above ground, such as the walls still to be found at Burgh Castle near Breydon Water. The walls here were gradually dismantled to provide materials for new buildings and were even used in the construction of nearby churches. The remnants were pulled down in 1747 and used for building materials, and the field in which they stood was ploughed up for agricultural use.

The natural harbours of the Burnhams were also undoubtedly known to the Romans. At that time there was a navigable, tidal waterway right up to what is now the village of Burnham Overy and beyond. Archaeological remains of several Roman trading communities and settlements, a number of which had at least one substantial building, have been found along the course of the old river. It is worth noting that the Romans were not the first to populate and work in the locality of Brancaster and the Burnhams. Evidence of Bronze Age and particularly Iron Age industry has come to light over the years in the form of coins, hoards, potteries, metalworking and even a torc, offering testimony to early settlement and wealth in the area.

In AD 410 the Emperor Honorius withdrew the last of his military units, leaving the occupants of Roman Norfolk to fend for themselves. Writing in the sixth century Gildas, the British churchman, said of the Angles' and Saxons' takeover, 'All the major towns were laid low by the repeated battering of enemy rams; laid low too, all the inhabitants – church leaders, priests and people alike, as the swords glinted all around and the flames crackled. . . . In the middle of the squares the foundation stones of high walls and towers that had been torn from their lofty base, holy altars, fragments of corpses . . . looked as though they had been mixed up in some dreadful wine-press. There was no burial to be had except in the ruins of houses or the bellies of beasts and birds.' It is thought the area around Brancaster and the Burnhams capitulated without bloodshed. Rather than falling as a result of enemy action many settlements were simply deserted and defences such as the coastal fort at Branodunum were left to rot.

Although archaeological evidence is scant it is highly probable that the Danes did infiltrate and merge with communities in the Brancaster and Burham area in the ninth century. Burnham Thorpe and Burnham Ulph can certainly trace the origins of their place names back to this influence. Ulph was a local chieftain

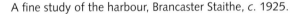

A fine study of the harbour, Brancaster Staithe, c. 1925.

bonded by blood to Canute. He is shown in the Domesday Book as holding some of the lands at Bumeha (Burnham), while Toki held lands at Bruneham torp (Burnham Thorpe) before 1066. By the eve of the Norman Conquest East Anglia was firmly back under Saxon control. From AD 969 the Lord of the 'Manor of Brancestre' was the Abbot of Ramsey in the Fens, who was also granted all profits of justice in Clackclose Hundred (a large area of south-west Norfolk), as well as money from Brancaster for clothing, food rent from Hickling and 60,000 eels from Wells. As Lords of the Manor after the Conquest his Norman successors held onto their lands until the dissolution.

The arm of the sea to Burnham was slowly silting up. By the thirteenth century it was not as wide as Roman sailors would have known it, but it was still wide enough to be navigated by the trading vessels that regularly sailed up to Burnham Rodested (between the mouth of the river and the present settlement of Burnham Overy) and beyond to Burnham Thorpe. This arm of the sea enabled the Norman church builders to bring up their stone and materials for the construction of the many fine medieval churches in the area. A monastic chapel was also founded at Burnham Thorpe in 1229 (nothing above the foundations remains of this building today). The first Carmelite house in the county was founded at Bradmere in 1241 and moved to nearby Burnham Norton in about 1253. It is at about this time that the preaching cross at Titchwell was also erected. In 1298 Walter, the son of the friary

The gatehouse and remains of the Carmelite friary at Burnham Norton, *c.* 1906.

founder William de Calthorpe, gave licence for a rood of meadowland to enlarge the house. A second enlargement followed in 1353. The chapel at Burnham Thorpe had been dissolved by 1500, but the Carmelite friary at Burnham Norton stood until the dissolution. Valued at £1 10s 8½d in 1538, its possessions were listed as 68 acres of land, '3oz of gilt, 58oz of white and a nutt garnished with silver'. The four friars who were left were said to be too poor to keep their friary in repair and wished to sell it. It is suggested the gatehouse and ruins that remain today may have been part of this second enlargement.

Both Burnham Thorpe and Overy were much larger and more densely populated than they appear today. The fine, large medieval churches in both these villages reflect the advantages they once enjoyed over the other Burnhams. Burnham Rodested/Overy Town was the larger; here business would be conducted around the Brothercross (from which the Hundred of the Burnhams takes its name) on the green. This was a thriving trading community that enjoyed a national reputation for the size and quality of its oysters, which at that time provided part of the staple diet of most people living close to the coast and its navigable waterways. Despite the port of nearby Lynn being in its ascendancy between the twelfth and fourteenth centuries, a healthy cargo of wool, wheat, oats and barley was exported from the Brancaster and Holkham Bay ports of Holme, Thornham, Brancaster Staithe and Burnham Rodested. Such was their affluence that even though the large local port of Lynn supplied four ships for Edward II's campaign against the Scots, Burnham still sent a ship of their own, as did Holkham. The trade of the ports was not without governance; one of the earliest appointments of officials here dates from 1568, when Francis Cobbes, Robert Jenyson, and Edward and William Russell were appointed deputies for the Commissioners for Havens and Creeks at 'Hunstanton-cum-Thoneham, Burnham-cum-Deepdale and Brancaster'.

A little aside worthy of note is the record of the great whales washed up along Brancaster Bay in the sixteenth and seventeenth centuries. During the reign of Henry VIII a message was sent post-haste to the King to act quickly if he wanted the great beached whale lest the 'grasping men of Thornham will soon remove it'. I bet the 'Merry Monarch' didn't see a scrap of it! In December 1626 another whale was cast onto the shore at Holme by a strong nor'westerly. It measured 57ft long and had a breadth from nose end to eye of 15½ft, 'the eyes about the same bigness as those of an ox'. In the mouth were counted forty-six teeth like the tusks of an elephant. The account concludes 'it was a male, had a pizzle [a penis] about 6ft long and about a foot diameter near its body. . . . The profit made of the whole fish was £217 6s 7d and the charge in cutting it up and managing it came to £100 or more.' In 1565 Elizabeth I's survey of the ports, creeks and landing places of Norfolk did not mention Brancaster or Thornham but noted Burnham Rodested as having two ships for carrying corn and coal, one of 30 tons 'burthen', the other of 42. In 1580 the ports of Holme, Brancaster and Burnham were all noted as ports with shipping over 16 tons, and they even applied to the Admiralty in 1630 for protection for their grain and coal ships, and ships that went to Iceland, against attacks from raiding 'Dunkirkers' and 'Ostenders'.

The bust of Admiral Lord Nelson, our nation's greatest maritime commander, in Burnham Thorpe Church. Born in the village in 1758 he sailed his first boats around the creeks of the Burnhams and Brancaster.

In 1642 Dutch engineers arrived at Thornham to build sea-defence walls and embankments. Distrusting 'foreign ideas' and fearing damage to their fishing 'the rascally people of Thornham' attempted to sabotage the day's work of the Dutch during night-time raids. Dogged by litigation Johannes van Haesdonke (also written as Hasedunck) petitioned the House of Lords, 'That he having in Order of this House, to quiet his Profession in some Fens in Holme, in Northfolk, the said order is disobeyed, his Corn spoiled, his ditches thrown down in a riotous and tumultuous Manner, and spoke divers contemptuous Words, and tore the Orders, as appears by an Affadavit.' Dutchman's Hill, the mound beside the shore road on the green, is one reminder of the work carried out in the area by van Haesdonke. By the late seventeenth century the Burn was more of a navigable river than an arm of the sea. It was far easier to offload goods at Brancaster Staithe and at the mouth of the river at Burnham Overy Staithe, where carts could collect goods and smaller vessels could transport light cargoes up the river to be stored in the large warehouse at Burnham Thorpe. This is well evinced by noting most of the extant old houses in Brancaster Staithe and Burnham Overy Staithe date from the late seventeenth and early eighteenth centuries.

After the enclosure of 1786 about 220 acres of salt marsh was embanked from tides, which formerly had flowed up nearly as far as the rectory at Titchwell. When the River Hun was diverted toward Thornham for marsh drainage Holme harbour silted up, to be effectively closed by the enclosure of the salt marsh in 1827, and trade came to Thornham. George Hogg, the man who had rebuilt and extended Thornham Hall after he took up residence there in 1788, built two granaries, jetties and a barn (used mostly for ale shipped up from London brewhouses). Hogg built his hall especially tall with a lookout on the roof so he could see when his boats were due, a feature he repeated when he built the Red House in the village. At Brancaster Staithe Elizabeth Savage is recorded as holding a licence for a pub named the Jolly Sailors in 1789 and in 1797 Burnham Market merchant John Thurlow erected a remarkable malthouse, claimed to be the largest in England. Blomefield described it thus: 'three hundred and twelve feet long and thirty one broad, wherein are steeped weekly in the season four hundred and twenty quarters of barley; this building is useful and handsome in its structure, and close to the quay for ships'. *Norfolk Tour* (1829) was so enamoured that it ventured to claim, 'Brancaster carries on the greatest malting trade in England.'

Trade in the Brancaster Bay ports was greatly reduced during the blockades of the Napoleonic Wars. Faden's *Map of Norfolk* (1797) shows the mouths of Thornham New Harbour, Brancaster and Burnham Harbours quite some distance from the actual staithes, leaving a tricky navigation for larger vessels, through drained marshland and silty creeks, to reach them. In 1822 local agriculturalist Henry Blythe funded the great bank from Burnham Deepdale to Burnham Norton, built to enclose 300 acres of marsh, but this did not improve the navigations to the harbours. The choking of these navigations by silt sounded the death knell for these small ports. By the 1830s the great malthouse was no longer the mainstay of Brancaster Staithe, which had returned to the old staples of coal imports and corn exports.

By 1846 bad harvests and the resultant agricultural depression saw corn exports greatly reduced, and records cease for a harbour master stationed at Brancaster Staithe. Matters were not helped here by the great embankment and improved harbour facilities constructed at Wells by the Earl of Leicester between 1854 and 1859. The final straw for the trading ports really came with the coming of the railway link to Burnham Market, opened on 17 August 1866. This line ran between Wells, Burnham Market and Heacham Junction and provided an easy link to the line

The Embankment, Burnham Overy Staithe, *c.* 1905.

The Market Place, Burnham Market, looking west, *c.* 1905.

to King's Lynn and ultimately the railway network across the country. The staithes of Brancaster Bay simply could not compete and, rather symbolic of those changing times, in 1878 the great malthouse built by John Thurlow at Brancaster Staithe was demolished. Thornham fought a valiant rearguard action by erecting a sluice at the turn of the century. The iron gate was wound down at high tide and raised when the creek was empty. It took two men twenty minutes to raise the gate. The resulting rush of water helped to keep the channel clear but it was simply not enough and the channel continued to need constant spadework. Admittedly, bargelike coal vessels known as 'billy boys' came to the harbours until just before the First World War, and the corn-laden farm wagons still stretched up Common Lane at Brancaster Staithe awaiting collection of their loads in the season. But by the 1880s their days as trading ports were ostensibly over.

Many local families were forced by the lean times of the 1830s and '40s to migrate to larger employment centres such as the port of Lynn, the growing industrial city of Norwich or even further afield, including emigration on the ships that left Lynn bound for the New World and Canada. Those who remained turned towards the home-grown industries of agriculture and fishing to earn their livings; some even turned to the old smuggling business. One account from November 1832 records a seizure of a tub boat at Brancaster found to contain 5,565lb of tobacco and about 650 gallons of brandy and genever by customs officers. Fishing had already been a way of life for some local families for generations, and the fishermen in this area had rich pickings. The oyster lays just off the mouth of Brancaster Harbour yielded 800 to 1,000 bushels of oysters during the season. Sea fishing had greatly diminished in this area by the 1850s so sprats, cockles and the acclaimed mussels proved the mainstays of the local fishermen's income.

Fishing families never forget the dangers of the sea, which can yield such a rich harvest and yet take its toll in the overturning of a boat and the crash of a wave. The local churchyards, especially Burnham Overy, are dotted with gravestones of those lost at sea; mute reminders such as the side-by-side memorial stones to brothers Samuel and Joseph Dowdy – both in their twenties, one with a young family – who were 'unfortunately' drowned on 25 October 1819. Severe storms were ascribed to witches even as late as the nineteenth century and were always said to 'blow in trouble'. During a severe gale on 30 August 1833 many lives were lost along this coastline. The Leith smack *Earl of Weymuss* went ashore at Brancaster. The heavy seas rent open the passengers' cabin, and six ladies, a gentleman and four children were drowned. Among the deceased was Miss Susan Roche, a young lady of great musical ability and the sister of the composer Mr A.D. Roche.

An inquiry into the causes of this disaster was opened on 16 October of the same year by the magistrates at Docking, under the authority of the Secretary of State, 'to ascertain for his own and the public satisfaction whether there had been any loss of life by culpable negligence or loss of property through dishonesty'. William Newman Reeve was committed to trial for removing 'certain property' from the wreck. Reeve's defence was simple – he was protecting it for his father, who was Lord of the Manor and had the right of wreck. He was acquitted without a stain on his character. At the Summer Assize yet another case for 'feloniously taking' from the same wreck saw Robert Allen, Charles Oakes and James Ward stand trial. The jury returned a verdict of not guilty for all of them.

There were already lifeboat stations at Hunstanton and Wells, but as more men turned to fishing in Brancaster Bay in the mid-nineteenth century, and no doubt influenced by the dreadful wrecks off the coast, a lifeboat was established at Brancaster in 1874. The men who served on the boat were notable for their longevity and loyalty to the service. The first Coxswain was Thomas Lane, who served his office for twenty-three years. His position was taken over by Robert E. Loose, who was Coxswain between 1898 and 1908. His place as Coxswain was taken by William Henry Loose, who saw out Brancaster lifeboat until the closure of the station in 1935. In sixty-one years this lifeboat was launched thirty-two times and saved thirty-four lives.

The sea can be a strange mistress, and the plentiful harvests of past years may not always be replenished. In the 1880s oyster stocks off Brancaster had diminished to the extent that local fishing families became so poor they could not afford shoes for children and the fishermen ended up working bare-legged, even in winter. Sheringham fishermen took pity on the men of Brancaster and the Burnhams and taught them how to catch whelks. It was to prove a golden egg. Sold to Yorkshire cod fishermen, who fished with long lines and required live whelks as bait, the rich catches at Little London, Haven Hole and Thornham Hole saw the fortunes of local fishermen restored to a reasonable living standard. The Brancaster Staithe fishermen

The Regatta at Burnham Overy Staithe, *c.* 1920.

never forgot their debt to the Sheringham men and wore the distinctive Sheringham gansey (a hand-knitted jumper) for generations afterwards.

Kelly's *Directory of Norfolk* for 1900 shows the diversification and innovation of this area after the decline of the harbours. There is no mention of a harbour or trading staithe, nor any fishermen listed at Holme or Thornham. Holme had returned to a focus on agriculture after the loss of its harbour in the nineteenth century, but was finding a nice little sideline in the holiday trade; Charles Bloomfield was listed as a bathing-machine proprietor and Albert Wales was offering apartments at Beach House. Further accommodation was afforded by a large tented campsite at Whitehall Farm. At Thornham a new industry had been established by the socially conscious Lady of the Manor, Mrs Ames Lyde. Begun in 1887 as an evening pursuit for villagers, designs were crafted by her brother-in-law, Victor Ames, and energetic encouragement was given to the project by Mr William Elsum, the schoolmaster. By 1894 two men were employed full time making gates, railings, balconies, hinges, fire dogs, and weathervanes. By 1899 they had taken over the premises of an old inn for offices and showrooms, and occupied two old cottages where seven forges were installed. There were five smiths, two bench hands and four apprentices; a total of twenty people were regularly employed at the foundry. However, despite notable orders from gentry across the eastern counties this wonderful enterprise never really paid its way. It ended with the death of Mrs Ames Lyde in 1914, though it didn't formally close until 31 July 1920. This failure notwithstanding, iron founding was not lost to the area. In the nineteenth century Powells of Brancaster had been established as a more practical enterprise, employing engineers, blacksmiths, iron and brass founders. After the First World War local men were taken on as this business grew to include agricultural implement manufacture, cart, van and wagon building, machinists and motor engineering.

In the mid-1920s there were something like fourteen whelk boats at Brancaster Staithe, which constituted the main fishing centre of the bay. The fishermen listed here in Kelly's *Directory of Norfolk* for 1922 were James Everitt, Herbert Winterbone, John William, Richard and William Southerland and Ernest, Henry, Henry Jnr, Thomas and William Henry Loose (who was also Coxswain of the lifeboat). Although a few hardy souls carried on harvesting mussels and shellfish at Burnham Overy Staithe, it was becoming far more of a haven for yachting and holiday boating to the degree that in 1922 John Stoker is listed as harbour master and fisherman and Richard Woodget as master mariner. By 1937 Burnham Overy Staithe offered William Haines, boat proprietor, Frederick Lane, boat owner, and entrepreneur Welcome G. Thompson, who was not only a builder and contractor but also a motor- and sailing-boat proprietor. The facilities were completed by Mrs Alice Toomey, who kept the Old Brigg Tea Rooms, Edward Fuller the confectioner, a grocery and post office kept by James Riches, and the Moorings Hotel. With all the new motor traffic along the coast road there was even Ben Allen the motor engineer. Indeed, the increased road traffic saw the section of the coast road in this area tarred in the 1920s, and there was even a bus run by Currys of Docking that took local folks to King's Lynn on Tuesdays for the market.

In the 1860s, in the days before tourism, the fishermen would squabble over the little bit of extra money they could gain from the pilotage of vessels into the harbours. At Brancaster Staithe the fishermen or their young sons would sit up on Barrow Common with telescopes to spot due vessels, and would race down to their boats to try and reach the ship first so as to be the one to navigate it into the harbour. When the railways and roads began to bring wildfowlers to this area, the fishermen found a far more lucrative sideline as the guns would pay well for their boat skills and local knowledge of good shooting grounds. In the 1920s, after the First World War, in which so many men lost their lives or their comrades, there was a distinct move away from shooting the birds to observing them and appreciating the natural beauty of the area; as one writer noted, 'the tweed-clad visitors brought far more binoculars than shotguns'. The sand spit between Brancaster Bay and Holkham known as Scolt Head Island was of particular interest and was only accessible only by arrangement with local boatmen. The majority of the island was purchased from Lord Leicester in 1923 by the joint efforts of keen naturalists Professor F.W. Oliver and Dr S.H. Long (the man who later founded the Norfolk Naturalists' Trust), and was taken into the care of the National Trust. When Charles Chestney was appointed full-time warden he built a sturdy keeper's hut and established a ternery where the sandwich, little and common terns nest.

Today the trading harbours of Brancaster Bay and the Burnhams are distant history, as in many ways are the old communities based around fishing and

Overy channel, *c.* 1912.

agriculture. Many of the cottages and houses have been bought as retirement homes or holiday cottages for incomers who do not raise their families in the villages. The houses and cottages they acquire are often restored or converted beyond the dreams of local folks a hundred years ago. Where once there were both fishing boats and pleasure yachts, the yachts now have the lion's share; the last boats to dredge have rotted away long ago and only a few people maintain the fishermen's craft. Whelk fishing here died out in the 1980s, but magnificent mussels and oysters have been restored to the bay; it is to be hoped that these will enable those hardy fishermen, whose families have worked these waters for generations, to keep on working here, maintaining their traditions and birthright for generations to come.

CHAPTER 4

The Glaven Ports

During the Middle Ages the Glaven ports were some of the most important trading centres of eastern England, but their existence was literally governed by the sands of time. Always endangered by encroachments of the sea, defences and embankments were constructed to keep back the waves, but these, combined with natural sand accumulations brought in by the ebb and flow of the tide, were to be the death of the trading ports of Wiveton, Blakeney, Cley and the satellite settlement of Salthouse, and could so easily also have proved to be the nemesis of neighbouring Wells.

Archaeological evidence shows that humans have lived in this area from prehistory onwards. The Iron Age fort at Warham, near Wells, is probably the most significant inhabited structure to survive in this area from that time. Pottery, coins and metalwork finds reveal a Roman and Saxon presence. Undoubtedly, sea trading was conducted here but there is little evidence as to the extent or the size of the settlements that existed before the Norman Conquest. At the time of the Conquest the villages and towns of Wiveton, Blakeney, Cley, Salthouse and Wells were already established, and their affairs were audited by Domesday Book assessors in 1086. But it must be remembered that these officials were more interested in making an inventory of land and property for tax purposes than in mentioning the extent or potential of sea trade. The villages of Wiventona (Wiveton) and Claia (Cley) were the largest settlements, situated about a mile apart on either side of a tidal estuary channel. Wiventona was the biggest with fifty-eight smallholders (which implied a population of at least 250) and two mills. The anchorages, with attached settlements of Esnuterle (Blakeney) and Salhus (Salthouse), were situated on navigable waterways behind the salt marshes that flanked the mouth of the estuary. Guella (Wells) had good settlement and provided a 'walk' for some 200 sheep 'and 4 beasts'; also noted was a mill, as was the fact that '24 pence of geld' could be rendered for tax between Guella and Warham.

By the time more specific records for maritime trade began in the thirteenth century, Cley, Wiveton and Blakeney were regarded as the only 'safe haven between King's Lynn and Great Yarmouth', and were established as leading ports in the area with a coastal and foreign trade based around fish. Unlike its haven neighbours, and despite having one of the earliest chartered markets in the area, dating from 1202, Wells had an unenviable reputation for wrecking which stuck with it for centuries

The old harbour and windmill at Cley, *c.* 1900.

afterwards, to the degree that the naming rhyme which ascribes traits or nicknames to local places included the term 'Wells bitefingers'. This cruel name is derived from the desperate stripping of dead bodies washed up after shipwrecks for anything of use or (especially) value, where the locals would literally bite or cut through the bloated fingers of the bodies to remove rings. One of the earliest of a number of cases brought against the wreckers of Wells in the thirteenth and fourteenth centuries was recorded in 1275, when a complaint was lodged by Thomas de Clare and Elias de Bebingham, on the complaint of John de Brilaund and his fellows (all merchants of London) 'that whereas a ship of theirs was laden with cloth and other goods at Calleys (Calais) and put to sea for Boston Fair, and anchored at Holcham, Co. Norfolk, some men of those parts attacked the ship and took away 304 cloths of wool, besides other goods to the town . . . and wounded some of the men in charge of the ship, some to death, and some by mutilating them . . .'. In 1278 it was recorded that John de Brilaund had obtained £300 'against divers men for goods taken by them in the parts of Holcham and Wells', but lodged a complaint that he had not yet been paid.

During the reign of Henry III, John de Blakeney, a King's Lynn fish merchant, was granted the manor in recognition of his services to the fishing industry. It seems that from this time the settlement formerly known as Snitterley, a derivation of its name recorded in the Domesday Book as Esnuterle or Snuterlea, became known as Blakeney. Both place names appeared in subsequent documents, and have provoked fierce debate over whether there was originally a separate settlement known as Snitterley that was later consumed by the waves. No archaeology, sea scour or diver has revealed physical evidence of Snitterley as another, separate settlement. Because both place names were used over the years I suggest it was simply a matter of Blakeney, the name so synonymous with trade and familiar to the hundreds of traders and merchants who used the harbour, gradually subordinating the old name of Snitterley, as opposed to a lost community swept beneath the waves.

Cley's market was formally granted in 1253; its port, along with that of Wiveton, had been larger and established at a time when Blakeney was just an anchorage. Hard though it is to imagine today, the lush, green valley between Wiveton across Newgate to near Cley Church was, in medieval times, a bustling harbour with wharves on both sides. Great trading vessels of well over 100 tons in size would berth here. Coastal vessels brought cargoes of coal, while the larger traders brought fish, wines, spices and cloth from the Continent, to be loaded for the return journey with wool and, later, woven goods for export. The landed goods would be taken away in tradesmen's carts or stored in one of several great warehouses that once stood here. There was a flourishing and well-established boat-building trade in Wiveton and enough trade wealth in Cley to establish a church there long before there was one in Blakeney. The great estuary channel to these ports led to a 'safe harbour', where there were purpose-built quays and facilities for bigger ships. There was even a chapel at Thornhams Eye, near the mouth of the haven, where monks and priests from Blakeney Friary would bless the boats setting out on their voyages and collect grateful tributes on their return. The ruins of this chapel may still be seen today; the old arch on the coast road through Cley is said to have come from this chapel.

By the fourteenth and throughout the fifteenth centuries Blakeney Haven (which comprised Blakeney, Cley and Wiveton along with the satellite settlement of Salthouse, connected to the haven by the Salthouse Mayne Channel) was one of the greatest ports in England. Here was a hub of foreign and coastal import and export, with Blakeney noted for its fish to the extent that in 1319 the King's merchant is recorded as buying 'herring, codfish, stockfish and Sturgeon' at Blakeney as well as at King's Lynn and Yarmouth. In 1326 Blakeney Haven is listed as the fourth name on a list of fifty-nine ports from which alone could be exported horses, gold, silver and ordinary money, because in the listed ports there were 'merchants sworn by oath to the king'. In 1310/11 the port of Blakeney had proudly supplied Edward II with a warship to be sent to Dublin to transport the forces raised there to Scotland. In 1335 another ship was demanded, but the locals thought they had been taxed enough. When the King's men came to collect the ship some local citizens 'forcibly entered the ship, sawed through and broke it up and assaulted the King's men'.

The affluence of the Glaven ports is well evinced by an almost continuous programme of additions, improvements and enlargement to their churches between the fourteenth and sixteenth centuries. Cley is notable for its monumental brasses (the marks on the floor belie the fact that there were once many more)

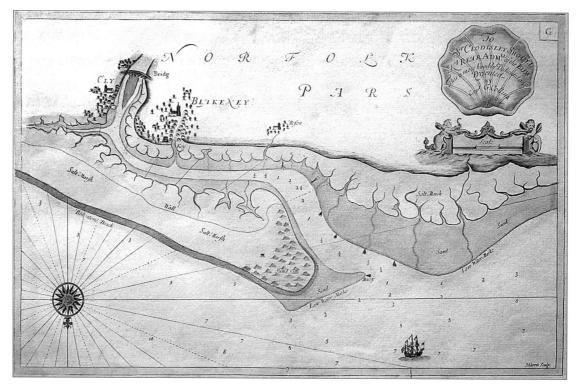

The Cley and Blakeney Sea Chart by Captain G. Collins, *c.* 1700.

and is particularly outstanding for the quality of workmanship in its decoration and construction. The magnificence of this church is undoubtedly due to the employment of John Ramsey, who came to prominence as master mason at Norwich Cathedral in 1304. John planned the building of a new and imposing church that included a new south aisle and clerestory. After his retirement in 1326 John's nephew, William, who was also a royal master mason, took over and built the north aisle and north transept. Cley Church eventually had two beautifully crafted transepts and four chapels until the schism with Rome. The works of John and William Ramsey on Cley were completed by the time the Black Death swept across Britain in 1348. The plague would claim the lives of both these master masons.

It is notable that Wiveton and Salthouse churches have more extant medieval graffiti that any other churches in the Glaven ports and for many miles around. Perhaps the creative fingers of the boat builders and sailors could not remain idle during the services. I like to think that the seamen, who were renowned for their skill in carving bones and tusks on their voyages, carved these small images of their boats with respect and reverence on the ancient walls in the hope that their vessels might also be blessed by a few of the prayers and hymns sung in those churches.

Blakeney Church, dedicated to St Nicholas, patron saint of seafarers, was begun in the late thirteenth century and was joined by a Carmelite friary founded in 1296, after 13½ acres of land was given over for the purpose in 1292 by John and Richard Stormer, Thomas Thober and other tenants of the Lord of the Manor, Sir William Roos. With his wife, Roos gave 100 marks towards the building of the church, which was consecrated in 1321, and something like eighteen friars took up residence in the friary. A notable feature of Blakeney Church is its fifteenth-century eastern tower, said to have been used as a type of lighthouse to indicate sufficient high water in the harbour for safe navigation and to guide ships into the harbour. In 1830 Blakeney Church was still noted as an important sea mark. At the top of its 104ft tower flags would be hoisted in answer to vessels in distress. This mark was said to be visible at sea from the Dudgeon, or floating lights, some 21 miles away.

The seventeenth century would be pivotal for the fates of the Glaven ports; the marshland and low-lying countryside around them were always vulnerable to incursions from the sea and liable to sporadic flooding, Cley Church register records no fewer than six 'rages of the sea' which did much damage in the eighty-four years up to 1749. As early as 1522 Sir John Heydon had begun works to change the flow of water in Cley Channel. In 1588 the north-west corner of Cley 'Eye' had an earthwork constructed for the observation of shipping in the wake of fears created by the Spanish Armada. It is interesting to note from a deed of 1651 that 'All that piece of high marsh ground in Cley aforesaid called or known by the name or names of ffoulness or East Eye conteyning by estimacon three score and ten acres' has been washed away by sea encroachments and today measures less than 30 acres. Encroachments at Cley and Salthouse are estimated to be up to about 3ft a year; in the seventeenth century the shingle beach of Cley lay several hundred yards north of

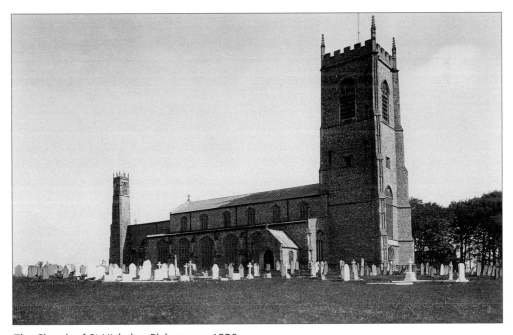

The Church of St Nicholas, Blakeney, *c.* 1920.

Newgate and the Church of St Margaret, Cley, *c.* 1910. Across this land toward Wiveton was once a sea channel and the bustling harbour of the Glaven ports.

the site of the present one and many of the old marshes, including most of the old Salthouse 'Mayne Channel' bed, have been overtaken by open sea.

On 1 September 1612 a disastrous fire gutted 117 dwellings around what is now known as the Newgate area below the church at Cley. The harbour had been gradually silting up over the years and the route was becoming dogged by a natural shingle bank that was continually extending westwards, so that when houses and stores came to be rebuilt they were constructed nearer the sea and the deep waters around the area we now know as the village of Cley. In 1630 Johannes van Haesdonke updated Heydon's works and began the process of draining the marshes at Salthouse. Within seven years Sir Henry Calthorpe and his son Philip were employing the same Dutch engineers on the drainage of Blakeney Marshes. The most controversial of all the embankments was the construction of a bank across the Glaven, which meant larger vessels would have to discharge their cargoes at Cley and goods would be transported overland to Wiveton. This situation led to the Calthorpes, after a protracted legal challenge lodged with the Port Court, being ordered to remove their obstructive bank in 1638. The judgment came too late, so that, by the time of its enactment, Wiveton had to all intents and purposes ceased to exist as a port and Cley's trade had halved.

For the next 200 years the harbours at Cley and Blakeney saw their international trade decline, to be used by coastal shipping, predominantly as the main export hubs for north Norfolk farm produce. Outgoing were the likes of barley, malt, fish and wheat to London and the ports of the north-east, while imports included staples such as coal, wine, linen and cordage, and 'specials' such as treacle, raisins, wine and pepper. Cley Custom House was built in about 1700. This area, like much of the north Norfolk coast, was rife with smugglers to the extent that Daniel Defoe commented in *A Tour Through the Whole Island of Great Britain*, published in 1724, 'From Clye, we go to Masham, and to Wells, all towns on the coast, in each whereof there is a very considerable Trade carried on with Holland for Corn, which that Part of the country is very full of: I say nothing of the Great Trade driven here from Holland, back again to England, because I take it to be Trade carried on with much less Honesty than Advantage; especially while the clandestine trade or the art of smuggling was so much in practice.'

In the early nineteenth century there was a hushed knowledge in Blakeney that anyone with a horse and cart who was in the know could go down to the quay on certain nights to earn a couple of shillings for running a few casks of contraband liquor for the smugglers. The quayside would be lined and stacked with barrels, but all had to be gone within about a quarter of an hour 'lest the excise men catch you'. As soon as the carts had rattled away from the quay and out of the town to find their cellars and hidey-holes, a few rapid shots of the preventive men might well be heard to ring out. Even if one wagoner was more tardy than the others the shots never seemed to hit their marks. The preventive men knew where the barrel was always hidden in return for their cooperation!

The revenue men did have their successes. In the winter of 1812/13 a smuggling cutter with some 600 casks of genever on board was captured off Salthouse by the Sheringham revenue boat. The vessel was taken to Blakeney Harbour and the cargo deposited in the King's warehouse at Cley. In December 1824 customs officers seized on the beach 120 half-ankers of genever, 19 bags of tobacco, 10 bags of snuff, 10 boxes of cigars and 2 Chinese ornaments, and lodged the goods in the Cley Custom House. In 'a desperate affray' on 26 February 1833 Lieutenant George Howes RN of the Weybourne Preventative Station and a party of coastguards under his command surprised a large number of smugglers at Cley. The smugglers put up a fearsome resistance and the coastguards were caused to discharge their weapons several times in self-defence. The haul they seized was, however, impressive: 127 half-ankers of brandy and 3–4,000lb of manufactured tobacco.

In the 1830s Cley was noted in *Pigot & Co.'s National Commercial Directory* as 'a place of little consequence in mercantile affairs, save what is derived from the importation of coals, and exportation of barley and malt . . . frequented in the summer season by many persons for the purpose of salt water bathing'. The directory's assessor could not, however, deny that 'a great deal of fine fish is caught on the coast by the inhabitants'. This view was further endorsed by a bumper harvest of oysters from the Cley beds in 1836, when 'many hundreds of tons' were caught; indeed the oysters were so plentiful that they ended up being sold to Kent dealers at sixpence a bushel. Blakeney fares a little better in *Pigot*'s; sea trade in oilcake, coals, timber and wool is noted, but with the codicil that 'trade is connected only with a few individuals, the inhabitants being chiefly sailors and fishermen'. Salthouse seems also to have fallen by the wayside as Cley and Wiveton declined.

Cley Street, 1904. The ancient arch on the building to the right is thought to have been removed from the chapel at Thornham's Eye, near the mouth of the haven.

The 'Salthouse Mayne Channel' was never the easiest of navigations and had been steered predominantly by inshore fishing boats. In 1790 the inward tidal movement of the shingle bank, which runs from Weybourne to Blakeney Point, accumulated to the extent that the channel connecting the waters of Salthouse Broad and Blakeney Harbour was blocked up. This reduced the movement of seawater at the eastern end of Cley Harbour. By 1850 this navigable waterway was completely blocked, and a new drain had to be dug out in 1855.

Although Cley did maintain sea-trading links into the early twentieth century, realistically, by the mid-nineteenth century the port was unviable and unsalvageable and jurisdiction was transferred to Wells in 1855 (a 250yd working quayside had been completed at Wells in 1853), with customs officials also being removed to Wells by the 1870s. When trade ceased at Cley, Blakeney enjoyed a resurgence in trade but the prosperity was short-lived. The railway arrived at nearby Holt in 1884 and offered a far quicker and more cost-effective means of delivering their goods all over the country. An ambitious plan was submitted by the Lynn & Fakenham Railway to buy out the Blakeney Harbour Company and construct a branch line from just north of Kelling to Blakeney Quay and on to Stiffkey and Morston. But careful consideration of the actual amounts of rail traffic likely to be generated by the line saw the idea abandoned in 1888. A similar end befell a proposed tramway from Sheringham via Weybourne, Salthouse and Cley to Blakeney Quay. The schemes were taken seriously, some land was purchased and a station master's house and office were erected on Lower Road in anticipation of the railway that never came.

In 1857, just two years after jurisdiction passed from Cley to Wells, the railway link from Fakenham to Wells was completed and the great embankment which assured the harbour a future well into the twentieth century was given financial backing by the Earl of Leicester, to be completed in 1859. Wells became the new sea-trade centre for north Norfolk. By 1904 a rail extension had been completed for goods wagons right along the harbour, and in 1906 the great gantry, the harbour's most eye-catching feature, was erected for the maltsters F. & G. Smith.

One man unfazed by the vagaries of sea trade in the Glaven ports was the magnificently named Onesiphorus Randall. Born in Cley in 1798 he made his fortune in speculative building construction in London that culminated in 1848 in the development of a 7-acre site into Randall's Estate. In the mid-nineteenth century he had obtained Kelling Old Hall, become Lord of the Manor and built a distinctive castellated lodge on land known as the Great Eye adjoining the beach at Salthouse. Randall enjoyed sailing and would find the house useful for his visits to the beach. He also thought it might provide a refuge for shipwrecked mariners. It was designed with tall and wide doors at either end of the building so that he could drive his horses and carriage straight through onto the flat grassland on

Salthouse windmill on the marshes opposite Grouts Lane, c. 1905. The mill, which ceased operation in the first decade of the twentieth century, had its top removed during the First World War as it was feared that the mill could be used as a reference point for Zeppelin raiders. The mill was demolished in the 1930s and the bricks were used in the construction of Ducklands at the bottom of the lane.

Tall-masted traders in Wells Harbour, *c.* 1900.

Blakeney Harbour in its last years saw tall-masted coastal traders, *c.* 1905.

Rebuilding and renovating the Blakeney embankment after the Black Monday storms which caused damage, sea breaches and flooding at numerous locations along the coast on 28 and 29 November 1897.

the seaward side, turn around and pass back through again. This building was nicknamed Randall's Folly and was sold to the Board of Trade after 'One's' death in 1873, to become a coastguard station where the rocket lifesaving apparatus was stored. After serving military purposes in two world wars the 'folly' met its nemesis in the 1953 floods when such damage was inflicted on the building that it had to be pulled down. Today most of the land that stood on the seaward side of the folly has been reclaimed by the sea.

For the latter half of the nineteenth and the early twentieth centuries Cley and Blakeney entered a kind of limbo, but local folks had to admit that the sea trade was over. A number of properties fell into dereliction and a number of the old warehouses were torn down. However, true north Norfolk folk are a very adaptable folk and not easily daunted, though it is true to say there were those who were too old or incapable of change who ended up 'on the parish'. For those able to adapt there was a fledgling trade in tourism that could be nurtured. Where once the tall-sailed traders had pulled up beside the harbour near the windmill, small pleasure sailing craft now began to appear and, rather like their comrades at Brancaster and the Burnhams, fishing boats were found to be quite adaptable for the purpose of taking visitors and wildfowlers out to Blakeney Point and around the salt marshes.

By 1890 only James Sands, James Fox, Robert Lewis and David Parlett were listed as master mariners in Cley, and Samuel Elliott acted as coastguard's boatman. Meanwhile, others turned their hands to diversification and what today we would call 'multiskilling': men such as Thomas Clarke, who was both bootmaker and

Pictured in Wells Harbour shortly before pall bearers carried them away for burial is a tragic reminder of the toll occasionally claimed by the sea; the flag-draped coffins of the eight sailors lost on the coal ship *Heathfield*, wrecked off Cley on 22 October 1910.

market gardener; or Frederick Stangroom, who acted as grocer, draper, ironmonger and chemist; or even Henry Nash 'Harry' Pashley, the landlord of the Fishmonger's Arms, also offered himself as a 'bird and animal preserver'. Harry's window of stuffed birds and tame white cranes were so renowned that Cley became a small Mecca for rare stuffed-bird collectors.

By 1881 the population of Blakeney stood at 804, almost 100 more people than at Cley. In 1890 trading with the sea and fishing remained the predominant business of the village. Edward Baines Snr and Jnr, Francis Kerrison, George, William and James Long, John Porter and Arthur Walker were all smack owners. William Bowles, Robert Butters, Alfred Digman, Robert Harvey, William Hook, James Mitchell, William Newland and Loads Thompson were all master mariners, and Robert Balding and Richard Starling were shipwrights. William Comber of Morston was the coastguard officer and Thomas Dew was employed as harbour master, collector of dues and deputy receiver of wreck. Similarly, there were still brewers, maltsters, timber, coal, cattle-cake and manure merchants in the village. Before the 1920s there was little or no tourist trade in Blakeney; it was scarcely mentioned in any visitor guide to Norfolk. Those who did visit tended to do so because they wished to visit Blakeney Point (and then the quickest way out was from Cley Quay by rowing boat). At the Point there was a renowned ternery. Here the visitor could observe the nests and feeding chicks in shallow depressions of the sand. Dr (later Prof.) F.W. Oliver had carried out extensive and valuable scientific work on Blakeney Point with colleagues and students from University College London. In 1912 the Point, its worth as a site of outstanding importance to geology, natural history and bird life having been established by Dr Oliver, was handed to the National Trust and became the first nature reserve to be established in Norfolk. Bob Pinchen was well remembered as the first National Trust warden. Shooting of ducks was still permitted 'for local tables' but was gradually phased out. Jane Hales relates a tale from the days when shooting was still allowed and a young lad impetuously shot a shelduck and took it to Bob to ask how to cook it (shelducks are quite inedible). The reply was typical of the countryman: 'Put you that in the oven along o' a brick, and when the brick melts the bird'll be tender.' She concludes intriguingly, 'The young marksman was to become a bishop.'

After the First World War moves were afoot to drastically change Blakeney. Sea trade was all but dead; Page and Turner, the last big corn merchants and mercantile traders, moved their business offices to Holt in 1922. This single event effectively extinguished the last burning embers of centuries of Blakeney as a trading port. Little comment was passed at the time because all eyes were on the transformation of Blakeney into an attractive holiday destination for gentlefolk. The old pub, the Crown and Anchor – known locally as the 'Barking Dickie' after the braying donkeys kept there – and adjoining buildings were demolished in 1921 and construction began on the superb Blakeney Hotel, completed in 1923 at a cost of £31,000 – quite a sum in its day. In high season in the 1920s accommodation in

Floods at Salthouse, 1938. The marshes and coast road are under water, but the Dun Cow and sturdy enclosure wall built as a safe haven for cattle from the marshes remains just above the water line on the left.

the hotel could be had for between 6 and 8 guineas per person per week inclusive of 'bedroom, attendance, baths, breakfast, luncheon, afternoon tea and dinner'.

In the early 1920s wildfowlers had a high time at Blakeney, Cley and Salthouse. During the winter of 1921/2, 852 head of birds were bagged at Salthouse alone, and that was in what was considered 'the worst wildfowl season for years'. In 1926 Cley Marshes were put up for sale by the executors of the late Arthur Cozens-Hardy of Cley Hall. Dr Sidney Long, founder of the Norfolk Naturalist Trust and the man who (with Professor F.W. Oliver) was instrumental in the preservation of Scolt Head and Blakeney Point, was anxious that this place so rich in bird life should be bought by the Trust and preserved for future generations and that 'certain of our lost species might be induced to return to nest'. A group of naturalists and bird lovers put up the funding and the marshes were secured. The first warden, or watcher, of Cley Marshes was Bob Bishop of Cley, who was succeeded by his grandson, Mr W.F. Bishop, in 1937, the same year the Norfolk Naturalist Trust purchased Great and Little Eye at Salthouse. Cley will always have the distinction of having been the very first county nature reserve in the country. It started a national movement of forty-seven wildlife trusts and over 2,000 nature reserves.

Today the area of the ancient Glaven ports is considered a place of outstanding natural beauty. Here are the classic wide-open skies of Norfolk combined with wind-whispered reeds, marsh, creek, nature and peace. There are echoes of greatness but no faded wealth. Here may be found solitude without loneliness. To me, and many others, there really is nowhere else like it in the world; it is truly one of Norfolk's most precious natural gems.

Across the marshes at Cley, *c.* 1910.

CHAPTER 5

Cromer, Sheringham & Poppyland

All the fishermen of this area are aware of the lost village of Shipden, which once stood on the seaward side of the town we know today as Cromer. The ruinous Church Rock just beyond the pier is a notorious sea hazard. On 9 August 1888 the pleasure steamer *Victoria* had set out on an unwise course from the pier when her hull scraped over Church Rock and was holed on her port side. Fortunately, she did not sink and all passengers were ferried off and sent home by train. Surely this is the only instance of a ship being stranded on the top of a church tower! William White stated in his *Norfolk Directory* of 1890 'At very low tides there are still to be seen, nearly half a mile from the cliffs, large masses of wall, composed of squared flints, which sailors call church rock.' Many is the time the hardiest of fishermen have cupped their hand to their ear to check the fabled bells of Shipden Church were not booming from their submerged belfry – if they were only a fool would go to sea that day, because a storm would be brewing.

Shipden is recorded in the Domesday Book with 2 free men, 5 smallholders and a total of 43 acres of land, 4½ plough, a meadow of 1 acre, land 'for the supplies of the monks' and woodland for 36 pigs. The assessed value for Roger Bigot, the owner of the lion's share of Shipden, was 10*s.* Cromer was not mentioned. As with many places swept away by time and tide their prominence often becomes exaggerated by folk tales and mythology as evinced by Pratt who wrote of Shipden's 'flocks, herds, spires, turrets and battlements'. Shipden was a typical north Norfolk trading port similar to those found around the Glaven. By the fourteenth century it was a well-populated town with a harbour and a number of manors, among them one owned by the Paston family and another in the possession of the Queen. The town had a number of fish-curing houses and even butchers, who would feed up the cattle which had been walked long distances on the nearby marshes before slaughter. Exports included a variety of locally caught fish, salt and barley, while imports ranged from Riga boards, timber and pitch to nails and coal.

Shipden suffered a constant fight with encroachments by the sea. By 1337 great chunks had been bitten out of Shipden, and its church, dedicated to St Peter, was abandoned to decay by the 1340s, while the trade of the village decamped to its landward satellite of Cromer. One of the earliest documents mentioning 'The merchants of Cromer' dates from 1358, and the construction of a new Cromer Church on the site of an earlier, smaller church began about this time. The church

The sedate clothing, parasols and bathing machines typify the genteel clientele of the East Beach, Cromer, in the late Victorian period.

reflected the wealth of the new, growing town and was dedicated to St Peter and St Paul, thus incorporating the names of the two churches of Cromer and its fast-disappearing neighbour. The fortunes of nearby Sheringham had also boomed with medieval sea trade, and their church was constructed at the same time. The bench ends in this church are remarkable: a baby in swaddling clothes, Nebuchadnezzar eating grass, and even a mermaid said by local folklore to be modelled from a real mermaid who would creep ashore and listen from the north door to the congregation singing.

The great storms of 1551 claimed the last of Shipden and smashed into the tall cliffs near Cromer. In the survey of ports and havens in Norfolk in 1565, Yarmouth and Lynn were the largest with over 500 households in each, but Sheringham and Cromer ran them a close third and fourth. It is interesting to note that Sheringham was the larger at the time, with 136 households and 69 fishermen to Cromer's 117 households and 48 fishermen. The fight with the sea was not over, and one of the earliest 'piers' in Cromer was a landing stage of a type recorded in Shipden as early as 1390. As the town was beaten back so each time the pier had to be reconstructed. Reconstruction was an expensive business and, as sea trade concentrated on the larger ports, the wealthy merchants of the town moved away and Cromer went into decline. Those who remained became resentful and fearful of those who traded on the sea, especially as many of those they had encountered from vessels were snatch squads of thieves and even pirates. In a *Verry Merry-Wherry-Ferry Voyage* (1623), John Taylor, the water poet, recounts his experience of a water excursion from Yarmouth, when foul weather forced him to land at Cromer. Frightened women and children immediately raised the alarm of raiders coming ashore! Parish constables were soon on the scene, swiftly followed by:

> Forty men with rusty bills,
> Some armed in ale, all of approved skill,
> Divided into four stout regiments
> To guard the city from dangerous events.

Taylor, the crew and his boat were placed under a guard. Obtaining lodgings at an inn he was interrogated under the gaze of curious natives:

> Besides, the peasants did this one thing more,
> They call'd and drank four shillings on my score;
> And like unmanner'd mongrels went their way,
> Not spending aught, but leaving me to pay.

Taylor was only able to leave after proving himself by reading excerpts from his works. Once his peaceable intentions were proved, his final hours in the village were hospitably entertained, and his boat was finally launched onto the calmed waters by the very people who had previously been so hostile to him and his crew.

The fortunes of the town, or rather the lack of them at this time, are well summed up by the rapid dilapidation of the church. With the wealthy merchants gone the endowments dried up and the building was soon too large and unmanageable for those who remained in the village. In 1681 the restoration of the chancel was estimated at £1,000. Permission was sought and granted by the Bishop to demolish this part of the church – one account suggested that the actual demolition was carried out by blowing the walls out at the foundations with gunpowder!

In 1724 Daniel Defoe visited Cromer and recorded his impressions: 'Cromer is a Market Town close to the shores of this dangerous coast. I know nothing it is famous for (besides being the terror of sailors) except good lobsters are taken on the coast in great numbers – carried to Norwich, and in such quantities sometimes too as to be conveyed to London.' Perhaps his allusion to the 'terror of sailors' came from hearing similar tales to that of Taylor, or perhaps, more likely, he referred to the infamously dangerous waters that lay beyond the town and down towards Happisburgh, namely the Haisbro' Sands, known to generations of mariners as the Devil's Throat. This forbidding name was well earned: in just one night, during the Great Gale of 1692, about 200 ships and over 1,000 people were recorded as perishing in the waters off Cromer.

At the time of the great storm the only warning of the dangerous waters was a large fire beacon on the north-west corner of the church tower. Strictly speaking the

BLACK SHUCK

The Devil Dog of the Coast

One of the most ancient tales to feature almost all along the Norfolk coast is that of the great, shaggy, black devil dog known by a variety of names – Old Shuck, the Shuck Dog and, the most popular, Black Shuck. Alleged sightings and activities ascribed to Shuck are particularly prevalent in the area between Weybourne and Overstrand, notably Shuck's Lane between Beeston and Overstrand. Said to date back centuries it has been suggested that Shuck is derived from the Saxon word *Scucca*, meaning 'devil'; perhaps, some have suggested, the dog was even a lost deity or demon of the ancients who no longer receives his supplication and veneration, and now lopes along the lane in chime hours to claim souls in retribution. The phenomenon of a black devil or demon dog is far from unique to this coastline; such beasts, known by different names, can be found all over the country. In Lancashire he is known as a Trash or Shriker, on the Isle of Man the Mauthe or Moddey Dhoo, in Wales he is the Gwyllgi and in Yorkshire it's the Padfoot. Each beast has been described as ranging in size from that of a calf up to about the size of a donkey. Most have very audible panting if you dare or are unfortunate to get close enough; his appearance is often accompanied by the smell of brimstone and fierce slavering jaws filled with sharp teeth. Some tales from the Cromer area state that the beast is headless, but that he still has a single eye, blazing like a coal from hell itself floating where his head should have been. It was said that anyone seeing this beast would have a member of their family (or indeed themselves) go mad or die within the year.

Like every other Norfolk coastal town (and most of the villages) there was a thriving business in smuggling in the Cromer area. While there is undoubted antiquity to the story of Black Shuck, the tale and accounts of his appearance had a resurgence in the eighteenth and nineteenth centuries when the tale suited the purposes of smugglers, who would send a pony disguised with a tattered black cloth thrown over it and a 'dark lanthorn' tied about its neck. Few locals would hang about to study the subterfuge close up if they saw that coming towards them in a country lane! One tale from the nineteenth century even tells of a local farmer playing a trick on friends he knew would be walking up a lane near his land after dark. He tied a lantern to the head of a large ram and attached a long chain, which came dragging and clanking after it. His friends' reactions are not recorded.

siting of the present Cromer lighthouse is in the parish of Overstrand, but the first considerations for a light were on a headland or promontory between the parishes of Cromer and Overstrand known as Foulness. Although Cromer had been identified as a suitable beacon site in 1549, Crawford Holden in *The Cutting of the Gem* points out that the village's first lighthouse was erected in 1669. One of five lights built along the coast as an experiment by Sir John Clayton, this Cromer light is said never to have been lit, because after lighting his lighthouse at Corton the ship owners refused to pay Clayton the dues he requested.

In 1719 Nathaniel Life, the owner of the land upon which Clayton built his 'blind' light, applied for a patent from Trinity House to erect a light on Foulness. This he did with Edward Bowel of Ipswich – quite whether they restored the old light or erected an all-new building is not clear – and the same year the new lighthouse of 'three moderate stories' surmounted by a coal fire blazing in an open hearth shone its first light. The fire was kept blazing by means of a large set of bellows worked by the lighthouse keeper, who was paid £50 a year for his troubles. In 1792 the lighthouse was fitted with a clockwork revolving light, one of the first of its kind in England. This lighthouse was subject to a number of near-miss cliff falls, notably that of 1799, which claimed half an acre of ground; the debris extended a considerable way into the sea at the low-water mark. Another fall on 15 January 1825 caused a breach in the cliffs of some 300yd, covering an area of about 12 acres. A great stream of water gushed out from the cliff after the fall, 'discharging itself upon the beach with great noise and violence'. There were no casualties, but the coastguard had a close call as they had passed the very area of the fall during the previous night! The final straw came early on the morning of

Fishermen line-baiting on the beach by the bottom of the East Gangway, Cromer, *c*. 1910.

A rare engraving by Ladbrooke showing the old and new Cromer lighthouses, 1833. The lighthouse to the right and headland on which it stood have now been completely eroded away by the sea.

19 August 1832 when another large shoot of the cliff occurred near the lighthouse. The masters and brethren of Trinity House deemed it expedient to build another lighthouse 250yd inland. The old lighthouse finally succumbed to a cliff fall during a fierce storm on the night of 5/6 December 1866, and with that the last of the headland of Foulness was washed away.

The lighthouse erected in 1832/3 is much the same building we can see today with its 52ft tower standing over 274ft above the level of the sea, and was lit with thirty colza-oil lamps placed in finely plated reflectors which revolved on an upright axis, presenting a full blaze of light every minute. Switched to Cromer town gas supply in 1905, it was finally converted to electricity in 1936. At its zenith the light produced a brightness of 100,000 candlepower and was visible for 23 miles out to sea. Remarkably, Cromer lighthouse maintained the same reflector-type optics of the old oil-fired lighthouse and was the last of its kind in England to do so. Cromer was the last permanently manned lighthouse on the Norfolk coast. Graham Fearn, the last lighthouse keeper, stepped down in 1990.

Another great maritime tradition in Cromer is its lifeboats. The first two boats were raised by public subscription in schemes led by local gentry motivated by the horrific loss of life at sea. The first resolution for such a boat at Cromer was passed at a public meeting in the town on 31 October 1804, and a local committee headed by Lord Suffield and Colonel Harbord set about raising a subscription. By the following January the remarkable sum of £700 had been raised and the first lifeboat was obtained. Just over thirty years later the Hon. Mrs Charlotte Upcher, widow of Abbot Upcher, the benevolent owner of Sheringham Estate, paid for the first Sheringham lifeboat, *Augusta*, named after the youngest of her children. The first RNLI lifeboat at Cromer, the *Benjamin Bond Cabbell*, arrived in 1858.

The second Sheringham boat was also funded by the Upchers and was named the *Henry Ramey Upcher*. Built by local boat-builder Lewis 'Buffalo' Emery, it was launched on 4 September 1894. The keel was said to be of 'an exceptionally perfect beam [of] American oak, without chick, knot or worm throughout its entire length'. Despite there being RNLI boats, the Sheringham lifeboatmen much preferred the *Henry Ramey*, which remained in private service until 1935. This lifeboat and her valiant crews were directly responsible for saving over 200 lives. It can still be seen, beautifully preserved and on display in Sheringham to this day. The RNLI closed the offshore lifeboat station in 1992, but in January 1994 Sheringham received the first Atlantic 75-class inshore rescue boat to enter RNLI service.

Cromer still proudly maintains its offshore lifeboat in a tradition that now dates back over 200 years. Many Norfolk lifeboatmen have been decorated or have been

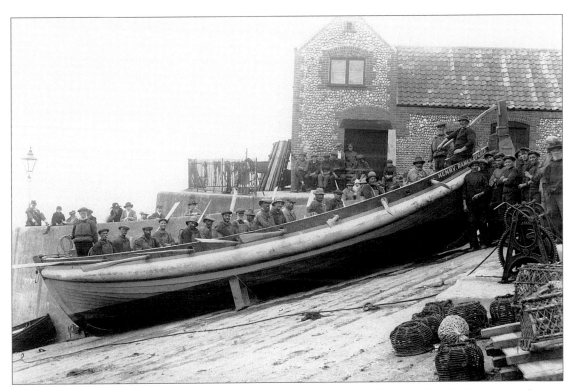

The crew and Sheringham lifeboat, *Henry Ramey Upcher*, in front of her boatshed on the fishermen's slipway, c. 1916. Known as the 'Fisherman's lifeboat' this row and sail lifeboat served for forty years and saved over 200 lives in 61 active launches.

The Cromer No. 1 lifeboat, *HF Bailey*, smashes into the water after its formal naming and launch by Lady Suffield, 26 July 1923. This lifeboat was the first to be housed at the end of Cromer pier in a specially constructed boathouse with slipway, which cost £30,000. This position and slipway enabled immediate launches into the sea in just about any weather, especially storm conditions which had previously been hazardous or nigh impossible with a shore-launched lifeboat.

given vellums for their gallantry – every recipient it has been my pleasure to meet has only spoken of their bravery with typical Norfolk modesty and reticence, most of them shrugging off their deeds with a twinkle in their eyes. I remember sharing a half-bottle of rum with the late Henry 'Shrimp' Davies (Coxswain of Cromer lifeboat, 1947–76) on a hot, sunny afternoon at his deckchair stall at the bottom of the West Cliff in Cromer before he would start to outline a few of his experiences. I knew not to press too hard; he named a few 'services' (the term lifeboatmen prefer to 'rescues') simply by giving the name of the ship such as *François Tixier* and *Georges Langanay*, which he thought would be of interest. He talked more of the men he served with, and shared many an anecdote and tale rather than any story of bravery. We shared so many laughs my sides hurt and my notes were almost illegible. I was particularly amazed to learn that most fishermen and lifeboatmen of old could not swim, but I learned one very valuable lesson above all. Every lifeboat crewman is special and, as any lifeboatman will freely acknowledge, a boat is only as good as the sum of its crew. Asked why he became a lifeboatman, the eyes of the old fisherman were deadly serious: 'If no one volunteered for the boat, who would be there if I needed help?'

Shrimp's uncle was Henry Blogg (1876–1954), and his outlook was just the same, but fate and his unique blend of personal gallantry, tenacity and leadership of his crews has marked him as the greatest of all the lifeboatmen; he was, as his memorial states, simply 'one of the bravest men who ever lived'. Henry was Coxswain of Cromer lifeboat for thirty-eight years, with fifty-three years' service in all. He joined the Cromer lifeboat in 1894 when he was 18, and was made Coxswain by the age of 33. During his years of service the Cromer lifeboat was launched 387 times and saved 873 lives. The actions of Henry Blogg and his crew, rescuing men from stricken vessels such as *Fernebo*, *Monte Nervoso*, *Sepoy*, *Porthcawl* and *English Trader*, have entered into lifeboat legend.

One of his most significant actions, the *Sepoy*, demonstrates the bravery of the Cromer crew and the quick thinking, instinct and judgement of Henry Blogg. This rescue occurred so close to shore that it drew crowds, and a famous series of photographs recording this dramatic action were taken by local commercial photographer Harry Hodges Tansley. It occurred on 13 December 1933 when the Cromer No. 1 boat, *HF Bailey*, was on service heading for Gorleston. The No. 2 boat, *Alexandra*, was launched twice, and both times the seas carried her back to the beach. The situation was looking desperate as, to the horror of onlookers, the *Sepoy* sank and the two-man crew climbed the rigging and lashed themselves to the mast. There was no radio on the *HF Bailey*, but a message was got to the

Launching the Cromer No. 2 lifeboat, *Harriot Dixon, c.* 1935. A tractor was not allocated this lifeboat until 1938, so she had to be hauled out at speed, by hand. The men on the forward ropes sometimes ended up to their necks in the water to launch the boat. There was some consolation; these men were paid additional 'wet money' of 1s. Those who only waded to their chests were given 'dry money' of 6d.

Coxswain Henry Blogg of Cromer lifeboat at the presentation of his second service clasp for his RNLI Gold Medal, presented by HRH The Prince of Wales at the RNLI's annual meeting at Central Hall, Westminster, 28 March 1928.

One of the most dramatic series of photographs ever captured on the Norfolk coast – the rescue of the crew of the 65-ton barge *Sepoy* which had been driven ashore 200yd off Cromer on 13 December 1933.

lifeboat via the secretary of the Gorleston lifeboat, who signalled the Cromer No. 1 boat. Blogg turned his vessel around and arrived at the *Sepoy* at 3.00 p.m. Despite the valiant efforts of *Alexandra*, her crew and local people who helped to relaunch her, and the firing of rocket lifesaving apparatus, the rescue attempts came to little avail. With winds howling and high sea rolling it was up to Henry Blogg to use all his skills, experience and intuition to make the right decision. He dared to drive *HF Bailey* over the sunken decks of *Sepoy* – an act he had to repeat twice, snatching a crew member on each pass! With the rescue complete but the lifeboat short of fuel there was no alternative but to drive for safety by beaching the boat on the Cromer shoreline. For his brave attempts at rescue, Bob Davies, who had been given charge of *Alexandra*, was awarded the official thanks of the RNLI on vellum. Each member of the crew of *HF Bailey* also received RNLI vellums and Blogg was awarded a second clasp for his RNLI silver medal. In total Henry Blogg was awarded the George Cross (the civil equivalent of the Victoria Cross), the RNLI Gold medal (the 'lifeboatman's VC') three times, three silver medals and the British Empire Medal. Henry respected the recognition he and his crews received but preferred to keep his medals in a box in the kitchen dresser than ever be seen wearing them.

In the early nineteenth century Cromer was principally inhabited by fishermen who earned their living by good catches of lobster, crab, whiting, codfish and tasty small herring. Frank Buckland's *Report on the Fisheries of Norfolk* (1875) states that crabs and lobsters were caught in 'hoop-nets', which were sunk to the bottom of the

Cromer 'Crabs', fishermen born and bred, *c.* 1902. Left to right: Bob Rix (with baby Emmerson), 'Ponsey' Harrison, 'Measles' Harrison (behind), 'One-eyed' Warner, 'Dirty George' Kirby, 'Billy' Davies, Mark Slapp and 'Will Doll' Rix.

sea and worked with the hand 'after the fashion of a minnow net' until the 1860s, when crab pots were introduced. Baited with 'butts' (flatfish) and other dead fish, the crabs enter the pots through two funnel-shaped doors, which act on the principle of a mousetrap. Once the pot has been hauled up, a side door can easily be let down and the crabs removed. Initially called 'floatums' at Cromer and 'swummers' at Sheringham, crab pots revolutionised the catching of crabs and it was not long before local fishermen had mastered setting a shank with several pots on it. Two crabs are counted as one, the two being called a 'cast', and six-score crabs were called a hundred – thus at Cromer a hundred crabs was actually 240. As Buckland points out, 'If one boat catches, in two tides fishing, ten casts of twenty crabs, it is considered a bad catch. A good catch would be three quarters of a Cromer hundred, or one hundred and eighty crabs.' In the latter half of the nineteenth century Sheringham and Cromer had about fifty crab boats a piece. Each boat was crewed by two men, and each carried about thirty to thirty-five pots. On a bad day 1,000 crabs would be landed at Cromer alone. It was estimated that during a good season, at the end of the nineteenth century, over a million crabs would be landed at Cromer.

Despite having no harbour a healthy sea trade was carried on at Cromer up to the late nineteenth century, with predominant imports of coal, tiles, oilcake and porter, and exports of corn. Vessels of between 60 and 100 tons from Newcastle, Sunderland, Scotland and the Baltic would lie on the beach, and at ebb tides carts were drawn alongside to unship the cargoes. When empty the ships would anchor a short distance from the shore to be reloaded by small boats or 'lighters'. *Norfolk Tour* (1829) noted that this was 'a measure attended with much inconvenience and expense, as the carts, though drawn by four horses, owing to the steepness of the road up the cliffs, can only carry about half a ton at a time. In this manner they continue passing and repassing till the water flows up to the horses' bellies, when they are obliged to desist till the return of the tide.' Colliers and similar craft regularly discharged their cargoes onto Cromer beach until the coming of the railway in the late 1870s.

A rare sight and a unique early image: three colliers, *Wensleydale*, *Commerce* and the *Ellis*, unloading their cargoes onto carts on Cromer beach, 1868.

A very fine study of the then newly remodelled Hotel de Paris viewed from the old jetty, Cromer, *c.* 1895.

The fortunes of the village of Cromer began to change in the late eighteenth century. The foundations of its tourist trade were laid when a select few gentry families, notably the Gurneys, Barclays and Hoares, chose to spend holidays enjoying the waters, scenery and 'good air' at Cromer. Their initial lodgings were on Church Street but soon more permanent residences were specifically purchased for the visits, such as Cliff House on Overstrand Road, bought by Samuel Hoare as his 'shooting box'. Thomas Fowell Buxton, Wilberforce's slavery-abolitionist comrade, rented Cromer Hall from the Windhams in the summer months. After Cromer Hall's fire in 1828 Fowell Buxton rented Northrepps Hall. Despite owning Colne House he loved Northrepps Hall so much that he made it his home and died there in 1845. Thanks to the 1811 improvements to the turnpike road from Norwich to Cromer, the coastal terminus soon became an exclusive and fashionable watering spot for increasing numbers of local gentry.

In 1814 Simeon Simons opened his hot and seawater baths at the base of the cliffs. Jane Austen was even moved to mention Cromer as 'the best of all the sea bathing places' in *Emma*, published in 1816. By 1820 there were nine commodious bathing machines. Lodgings, inns and hotels rapidly expanded and improved to accommodate their 'polite' clientele. One of the first was Tucker's New Inn and Family Hotel on Tucker Street, as well as the Lion and the Wellington Inn, which offered some of the best private lodgings in the town. Lord Suffield sold his cliff-top summer residence to Pierre le François in 1830, and the Hotel de Paris was developed on the site. The foundations of a great seaside destination had been laid, and between 1801 and 1845 the population of Cromer rose from 676 to 1,270 inhabitants, most of them supporting the holiday trade or the expanded infrastructure.

The latter half of the nineteenth century was to be truly the cutting and polishing of Cromer as 'Gem of the Norfolk Coast'. Railways came comparatively late to Norfolk. The first line to stretch towards Cromer was proposed by Lord Suffield in 1863; the East Norfolk Railway line was initially intended as a link between Norwich and North Walsham, but the only way to raise the capital required was to promise an extension to Cromer. Norwich to North Walsham was completed in 1874 with the Cromer link opened in 1877. The timing in many ways could not have been more opportune. A new, affluent middle class had emerged from the Industrial Revolution. Rising above the labouring working class, these were the likes of educated clerks, artisans and managers, who headed households maintaining manners, morals, 'respectable behaviour' and standards of living which had only been available to the wealthiest families two or three generations earlier. This new, more affluent generation sought to spend their public holidays away from the old focal point of the pub, and get away from 'the smoke' for a trip to the seaside, even if it was only for one day. The railways made this journey possible, with east coast expresses running direct from London's Liverpool Street to Cromer on a journey that could be achieved in 2 hours 55 minutes.

Cromer was already popular, but the phenomenon which changed the coastal town and its district into a Mecca began on 30 August 1883, when Clement Scott published the first of his *Poppyland* columns written 'by a holidaymaker . . . at a farmhouse by the sea'. The somewhat sentimental accounts of his idyllic experiences at the miller's cottage, with old miller Jermy and his pretty daughter Louie, the farm animals and country life, contrasted with his vivid word pictures of genteel visits to the seaside and the nearby countryside or strolls along the

Clement Scott (1841–1904), the man who created 'Poppyland'.

Mill House, Sidestrand, *c.* 1910, the chance discovery of Clement Scott and immortalised in his *Poppyland* writings 'by a holidaymaker . . . at a farmhouse by the sea', in the *Daily Telegraph*, 1883.

cliffs, appealed to the readership immensely. But his flowery prose for *Poppyland* and *The Garden of Sleep* were what really captured the public's imagination. Poppyland was the name Scott gave to the fields perched along the cliff tops between Sheringham and Sidestrand, which swayed with the distinctive red blooms in the summertime. The spiritual heart of Poppyland was the ruined tower of Sidestrand Church, which stood like a gaunt sentinel juxtaposed with the cliff edge, its ultimate fate of falling and smashing just feet away, with poppies garlanding the old gravestones nearby:

> In my garden of sleep, where the red poppies are spread,
> I wait for the living, alone with the dead!
> For a tower in ruins stands guard o'er the deep,
> At whose feet are green graves of women asleep!
> Did they love as I love, when they lived by the sea?
> Did they wait as I wait, for the days that may be?
> Was it hope or fulfilling that entered each breast,
> Ere death gave release, and the poppies gave rest?
> O! life of my life! On the cliffs by the sea,
> By the graves in the grass, I am waiting for thee!

Excerpt from *The Garden of Sleep*, Clement Scott (1885)

A classic image of the ruined tower of Sidestrand Church, eulogised and popularised by Clement Scott who christened it 'The Garden of Sleep' - the heart of his 'Poppyland'.

Overleaf: The smart walks along the East Cliff, Cromer, 1898. This rare view was taken between the time when the old jetty was severely damaged and cleared away in 1897 and before construction began on the new pier in 1899.

By the Seaside

Poppyland and Cromer were described in the following manner in the *Ward Lock Guide to Cromer and District*, for the season 1905/6:

Sidestrand, the tiny parish on the cliff 'discovered' by Mr Clement Scott, and made famous by him under the name of 'Poppyland'. There is the manner of an explorer in his pleasant account of how he rambled away from the Cromer holiday-makers 'digging on the sands, playing lawn tennis, working, reading, flirting and donkey riding' and reached 'The Cottage by the Mill' where he found comfort and peace and happy days. 'It was', he writes, 'on one of the most beautiful days of the lovely month of August. A summer morning with a cloudless blue sky overhead, and a sea without a ripple washing on the yellow sands', that he turned his back on Cromer and wandered over the heather downs beyond the lighthouse. At Cromer, 'it was the rule', he continues, 'to go on the sands in the morning, to walk one cliff for a mile in the afternoon, to take another mile in the opposite direction at sunset, and to crowd upon the little pier at night. . . . No one thought of going beyond the lighthouse; that was the boundary of investigation. Outside that mark the country, farms and the villages were as lonely as in the highlands.'

The account concludes on lodgings in Poppyland. 'Farmhouses empty, cottages to let, houses to be hired for a song'. Thus we read in the prose idyll which has made this region known to the holiday-making world. But things have altered; cottages and farmhouses are no longer 'to be hired for a song' and so popular has the district become, that it is a difficult thing during August and September to find lodging accommodation of any kind.

In 1905 a First Class 'Tourist' return fare from London to Cromer was 34*s* and 3rd Class was 20*s*. The Grand Hotel would cost 10s 6*d* per day or 70s per week whereas the Marlborough Private Hotel offered the same day rate as the Grand but the cut price 52*s* 6*d* for a week-long stay. For your days at the beach 'covered accommodation' was offered at 6*d* a day per person or 5s for a dozen tickets; adverts emphasised 'Mixed bathing is permitted'.

The view across the East Beach from the jetty, Cromer, *c.* 1895. To the right of centre on the prom is the three-storey Lower Tucker's Hotel where the Empress Elizabeth of Austria stayed in 1887. Above left of Lower Tucker's is the now-demolished Hotel Metropole.

The Garden of Sleep struck a chord with every household which had a 'Nearer My God to Thee' scripture card or a Landseer print on its wall, to the extent that thousands wanted to experience Poppyland for themselves.

Cromer had only been linked to the railway a few years and was far from developed for the holiday trade. Many considered its beauty unspoilt, unlike other rail-linked resorts such as Blackpool and Bognor, which attracted 'too many trippers' and vulgar beach entertainments such as Punch and Judy, hawkers and minstrels. Because of the lack of adequate hotel space or rented accommodation its clientele had to be wealthy, and thus the clientele remained pretty exclusive. Because much of the land around Cromer was part of the Cromer Hall Estate owned by Benjamin Bond Cabbell, it was not available for sale and development except for a few portions of land along Norwich Road, which were sold with the codicil that the buildings constructed would be exclusive villas and lodgings. However, so many people were keen to stay in Poppyland that the nearby villages of East and West Runton, as well as Sheringham, rapidly began to benefit from the overspill. At West Runton the Links Hotel was erected in 1890. After the death of Benjamin Bond Cabbell larger portions of estate land around Cromer were sold off and the great hotels along the West Cliff, such as the Grand (1891) and the Cliftonville (1894), came to prominence, along with the magnificent Metropole, designed by leading Norwich architect George Skipper, on Tucker Street. Hotels like the Hotel de Paris and the Marlborough were extended and improved beyond recognition, with new frontages, grand entrances, towers and cupolas. Patronage of the locality was also important; Poppyland saw regular visits by bohemians and poets like Algernon Swinburne and his friend Watts Dunton, the famous columnist George R. Sims, and notable actors and actresses such as Henry Irving, Herbert Beerbohm Tree and Ellen Terry. Even Arthur Conan Doyle, the creator of Sherlock Holmes, came to stay. He heard the legend of Black Shuck, the devil dog of the coast, and was inspired to write *The Hound of the Baskervilles*. The cachet of Cromer was finally sealed, in those halcyon days before the First World War, by royal patronage, with a residential stay from Empress Elizabeth of Austria in 1887 and other members of the German nobility throughout the 1890s.

By 1900 Cromer was firmly established as the most popular of Norfolk's coastal destinations for gentlefolk, the surrounding villages were building hotels and lodging houses, and re-fronting old buildings to appeal to the new holidaymaker trade. Cromer now had two stations; the oldest, dating from 1877, had been taken over by the Great Eastern Railway and became known as 'Cromer High' because it was over a mile away from the beach, on Norwich Road. The other, Cromer Beach station, had been opened in 1887 on the M&GN, bringing visitors and holidaymakers from the Midlands and north of England to Cromer. It was also in 1887 that the M&GN extended its branch line from King's Lynn and Norwich via Melton Constable to Sheringham.

The Lobster Coach, complete with its liveried driver and well-turned-out passengers ready for the off from the Grand Hotel, Cromer, *c.* 1910.

Sheringham West Beach at the bottom of the West slipway, *c.* 1895.

Although Sheringham village had enjoyed overspill from Cromer and visitors in its own right, its real commercial success only came with the arrival of the railway. While the old village of Upper Sheringham remained almost unchanged, the fishing hamlet of Lower Sheringham by the sea was rapidly transformed from a fishing hamlet to a village and then to a coastal resort town. Old dust-track roads were metalled and given pavements, and old shops and businesses were afforded new, impressive frontages. St Peter's Church was built between 1895 and 1897 for the growing town and its visitors. New roads, a boulevard, houses, guesthouses and the great hotels – the Grand, Burlington and Sheringham – were all built at a remarkable pace in the 1890s. The crowning moment of all the improvements and development of the new Sheringham resort came in 1901 when it was given responsibility as a self-governing urban district.

Particular consideration was given to the development of the seafront from a sandy gap for fishermen into a series of flint-walled sea defences with a fine promenade. By 1896 over £30,000 had been expended. By 1900 the sea wall and promenade extended for two-thirds of a mile, increased by 113yd on the eastern side in 1909. Although, the *Ward Lock* guide to the district in 1907 commented rather harshly, 'The Promenade is not stately, and makes no pretence of beauty. Truth to say, it is a trifle dingy . . .', I am sure the good councillors of Sheringham would have argued practicality and sturdiness over beauty – especially after the sea encroachments noted in later editions of the guide. In 1829 'there was a depth of

Sheringham High Street, *c.* 1910, is unrecognisable from the rows of fishermen's cottages which stood here forty years before.

twenty feet, "sufficient to float a frigate", at one point in Sheringham Harbour where only 48 years before, there stood a cliff fifty feet high with houses upon it.' The account concludes with the poignant note, 'The flagstaff of the Preventive Service station (on the sea front) has been thrice removed inland in consequence of the advance of the sea.'

Cromer had erected defensive walls and breakwaters in wood and stone for generations. The first work of more modern times was the construction in 1836–8 of a sea wall with a narrow grassed promenade. This was overlapped by a further wall built to protect the western half of Cromer. The first stone of this wall and esplanade was laid by the Revd W. Sharp, and the first pile of the new jetty was driven in, in April 1846 (the old jetty had been washed away the previous year). These works were quickly completed at an expense of about £7,000 and were opened amid much festivity on 7 August in the same year. In 1894 a wall and esplanade was built at the foot of the East Cliffs, while new approaches were built opposite the jetty and a bandstand was erected. In 1897 the jetty was severely damaged in a storm and dismantled for safety. In 1899 an Act was granted for the construction of the pier. Measuring some 500yd long, it was designed and built by engineer William Tregarthen Douglass for the sum of £17,067 14*s* 5*d*. Douglass also designed and oversaw the construction of the sea wall and the continuation of the promenade to connect the Eastern and Western Esplanades into one long promenade, for the grand sum of £34,000.

Cromer Pier was opened on 8 June 1901 by Lord Claude Hamilton, Chairman of the Great Eastern Railway Company. When the pier first opened, 1d was charged for admittance with 2d extra to enter the bandstand enclosure at the pier head. This area was covered over and developed into the Pavilion Theatre between 1905 and 1912. Despite suffering severe storm damage (especially during the 1953 floods), having its middle blown out by explosives in 1940 as an anti-invasion measure, and being bisected by the Tayjack rig which had shot its lines in a storm, the pier has been lovingly maintained and restored for over 100 years and proudly hosts the longest-running summertime pier show in the country.

Whereas the towns of Cromer and Sheringham and their surrounding villages had a tourist trade which had grown somewhat organically through the nineteenth century before enjoying a meteoric rise in popularity through the general public's imagination, desire and ability to experience the dream of Poppyland, the further development and, if we are to be frank, the stretching of the boundaries of Poppyland to Mundesley was purely a financial speculation between the railway and property developers. The ideas were grand: a new holiday resort town built on the West Cliff was to be called Cliftonville. Plots of land were put up for sale in 1890 and two new hotels were built – the Clarence and the Grand – soon to be followed by a third hotel, the Manor House. The warning signs must have been obvious. Few of the plots of land for Cliftonville

The old jetty and East Beach viewed from the cliffs, Cromer, *c.* 1894.

The original Cromer Pier of 1901 with iron gates, kiosks and covered bandstand and seating at the pier head.

Cromer Pier, with shelters and kiosk moved to the middle of the pier near the Pavilion Theatre, *c.* 1935. The theatre had been developed from the old bandstand and seating between 1905 and 1912.

A fine study of the railway station at Mundesley, shortly after it opened in 1898. The dream of Mundesley and Cliftonville was never realised; the visitors seemed unable to stretch to such numbers and the final trains left Mundesley in 1964. As the tracks have been taken up and the buildings and platforms demolished there is hardly a trace of the former railway station.

Cromer Road crossroads, Mundesley, c. 1910.

West Runton Common and the grand Links Hotel, built in 1890, *c*. 1908.

were sold and, even with the coming of the railway in 1898, the anticipated trainloads of visitors never came in the same numbers as those who heaved into Cromer and Sheringham stations. A further rail link completed in 1906 saw a loop of rail run from Cromer via Trimingham and Overstrand back to Cromer. Despite there being hotels, boarding houses, golden sands, bathing machines, swing-boats on the beach and a fine promenade by 1908, the visitor numbers never burgeoned.

Clement Scott saw his numerous *Poppyland* articles collected and published in book form in 1886, to be reprinted on several subsequent occasions under various titles. Other writers followed his themes, and not only a holiday industry but also 'Poppyland' merchandise such as perfume, china, postcards and even sheet music developed from Scott's initial 'discovery'. But, in the days before advanced artistic rights, Scott was only ever paid for his writings and received little or no commission from the spin-offs developed by others. Cromer had expanded beyond his wildest imaginings; Sheringham was a coastal resort town in its own right, and villages like West and East Runton had become unrecognisable from the hamlets they had been just a generation before. Sidestrand had not become overdeveloped, but its once-sleepy neighbour of Overstrand had become the exclusive home of some of the coast's most wealthy visitors. A number chose to build their huge homes in the village, to the extent that it became known as the 'Village of Millionaires', with no fewer than six such wealthy people living in a community of just 400. In 1890 Scott expressed his regrets: 'The Cromer that we visit now is not the Cromer I wrote about a few years ago as my beloved Poppyland.' He felt he had doomed the area to become 'Bungalow Land', and in many ways he wished he had kept his thoughts to himself or had never revealed

By the Seaside

The facilities and experience of a trip to the seaside at Sheringham are described in the *Ward Lock Guide to Cromer and District* for the season 1926/7:

> The firm and clean sands and the gradual slope of the beach make bathing at Sheringham pleasant and safe. Mixed bathing is allowed; and in place of the ordinary bathing machines are long rows of 'box-tents' fitted with a wooden floor and provided with lock and key, by which the bathers may keep in safe custody the conveniences required for a 'dip'. In these 'tents', too, are kept the tea cups and saucers, the spirit lamp and kettle, and other accessories of the high function of 'afternoon tea'. In the cliffs the council have erected chalets which are convenient for bathing, and, being at some height above the promenade, afford a splendid view of the beach. The Sheringham beach forms a delightful and unconventional picnic ground. Protection boats, provided by the council, are always present, and it is noteworthy that there has never been a bathing fatality at Sheringham.
>
> For the 1926/7 season a week-end train ticket from London to Sheringham cost 34/9 first class or 21/- third class. A stay at Sheringham Grand cost 16/6 per day or 115/6 per week or at Woodford Guest House 12/6 per day or 73/6 per week.

Sheringham Beach, West Promenade, 1904. Shown are the traditional three lines of tents from the Upcher Groyne to the steps down the cliff from the Grand Hotel and beyond. The tents below the Grand, which were used by the guests at the hotel, always attracted the highest premiums.

the true names of the places, that made up Poppyland. Clement Scott died in 1904, and it was over five years before any monument was erected to the man who had 'made' the area. Even then it was no bust or tastefully prominent plaque but a drinking trough with separate bowls for people, horses and dogs – those who erected it referred to it as a 'fountain' – beside the road leading from Cromer to Overstrand and Sidestrand.

With Scott's death, in many ways Poppyland began to die too, the victim of its own success and the financial speculation of Cliftonville at Mundesley, which was simply not to be. Times were changing and the genteel world of Victorian and Edwardian life and holidays was shattered in 1914 by the outbreak of the First World War. Two years later thousands of those young gentlemen who had walked innocently arm in arm with their sweethearts and fiancées among those romantic fields of poppies and the 'Garden of Sleep' already lay dead on the fields of France and Flanders. On 26 February 1916, as the plans for a 'Big Push' on the Somme were being formulated, the church tower of the Garden of Sleep slipped, unwitnessed, over the edge of the cliff and smashed onto the beach below. On 1 July that year, the first day of the Battle of the Somme, the British Army suffered over 57,000 casualties. Many had said in the years before that Poppyland would end when the tower fell. Like the tower, a generation fell that was never to be. The irony was not lost on many when poppies flowered 'between the crosses, row on row' in Flanders fields. Nothing was ever the same again.

Once the seaside resorts took off the opulent style of the new Cromer and Sheringham buildings spread to the hamlet in between; no more is it more clearly shown than here on East Runton High Street, c. 1900. The new-style buildings can be seen on the left and the old flint-faced ones of the fishing hamlet are on the right.

CHAPTER 6

Bacton to Winterton – Where the Sea Claims its Toll

With the exception of the high ground and cliffs around Happisburgh, this stretch of the Norfolk coast consists mainly of low dunes and marrams. Compared with all other areas along our county's coastline it is here that erosion is at its worst and encroachments by the sea are most common and dramatic. Geographical features have been claimed by the sea here, but also entire towns and villages that now only exist as hamlets or scattered communities. It is here that the sea now indefatigably laps at the boundaries of several villages and significant structures that were once miles inland, and poses an ever-present threat to claim yet more. In the mid-fourteenth century 4½ acres of good land was lost to the sea just on one stormy night. It was reckoned that between the 1780s and the 1840s one of the villages in this area had lost as much as 50 acres. Combine this with the notorious Haisbro' Sands, which extend 9 miles off the coast here, its neck off Cromer having been known to generations of mariners as the 'Devil's Throat', and it is clear that this stretch of sea has been a wrecking ground for many poor ships and a watery grave for many sailors. Along this stretch of coastline, above all others, it may truly be said that the sea claims its toll of both land and shipping.

We begin our journey in the village of Bacton, a pleasant seaside community which benefited from being on the fringes of Poppyland and maintains an economy based around the holiday trade with its caravan park, small amusement arcade, shops and pubs. Sadly, the outlying beach of this village now lies in the shadow of a major North Sea gas terminal.

Bacton was once one of three settlements – Bacton, Keswick (spelt in early documents as Keswic) and Bromholm – which clustered here. Keswick is thought to have been a small town with a healthy sea trade. It was certainly recorded as having a fine church dedicated to St Clement quite some distance inland but the sea's encroachments gradually worked their way up to the old church and severely damaged it during a great storm in 1382, and the ruined church was abandoned for religious purposes and used as a grain store.

Further inland was the religious house and community of Bromholme. The priory was founded in 1113 as a Cluniac cell of the priory at Castle Acre. The fate of the

Happisburgh lighthouse and cottages, 1907.

The Fisherman's Gap, Bacton, *c.* 1920. Most of these sandy 'Gaps' which wound through gaps in the cliffs or dunes, once so common to fishing communities along the Norfolk coast, have now disappeared because of coastal erosion, improvements for visitors and sea-defence schemes.

priory could well have been a quiet existence had it not been for a portion of the True Cross that they claimed to possess which was said to perform miracles. The Holy Rood of Bromholm was alleged to have raised no less than thirty-nine people from the dead and restored the sight of nineteen. The priory's fame entered into popular parlance and the exclamation of 'Oh, Holy Rood of Bromholm' appears on a number of occasions in early English literature including *Canterbury Tales* (in *The Reeve's Tale*) and *Piers Plowman*. The priory was a major centre for pilgrimage in Norfolk until the dissolution of the monasteries in 1535, when the monastic buildings were left to rot. The steadily decaying ruins and the land all around that had been put to cultivation made real the ancient prophetic couplet:

> When Keswic church becomes a barn,
> Bacton Abbey will be a farm.

And so they remained until 1761, when the remnants of Keswick church which had not been incorporated into farm buildings were taken down. The bones of those who had been laid in the cemetery were unceremoniously disinterred and carted away a few years later when the churchyard was cleared to allow the beach road to be driven through it.

The interests of those who relied on shipping for their wealth and those who had been shocked by the loss of life off this section of coast led to fund-raising efforts to

Coastguard House and Rocket Brigade, Bacton, *c.* 1905.

get Bacton a lifeboat in the early nineteenth century. They were joined by a keen band of beachmen who would look after basic life-saving and attend to wrecks that were beached. The coastguard station was manned by a chief officer and four men; they were also equipped with one of Manby's apparatuses, which could fire rescue lines onto distressed vessels by means of a gun on the shore. Sadly, the tiny village found it difficult regularly to turn out a full crew for the boat, and she was transferred to Caister. However, the Caister men refused to use the vessel and returned it to Bacton, where it was taken under the wing of Robert Cubitt, the Superintendent of Lifeboats, who not only brought the boat up to seaworthy standard but also enlarged the vessel and did much to foster an active crew. The RNLI took over the station in 1857, paid for a new, self-righting boat and in 1858 erected a new boathouse. The old boat was given to the Bacton beachmen, who continued to use it until the 1880s.

One particular 'service' given by the new lifeboat, of which they were very proud, was still noted in the entry for *White's Directory of Norfolk*, published in 1890, which related that the 'crew displayed great bravery during the terrific gale of December 1863 when they rescued the crew of the barque *Ina*'. In February 1880 the RNLI presented Mr William Partridge Cubitt jnr (1854–1929) with their highest award, the gold medal, for his bravery in cutting a rope which had become entangled in the rudder and capsized the lifeboat. Although two of the boat's crew had been killed instantly, if Cubitt had not acted so quickly and decisively the rest of the crew would have suffered the same fate. Mr William Cubitt snr was convinced that the capsize was due to a design fault in the self-righting boat and resigned from his position of Honorary Secretary of the Bacton lifeboat. The crew lost confidence in the boat and the RNLI inspector recommended that the lifeboat station be closed – and so it was in 1882. The boats and crews of this often forgotten lifeboat station are credited with saving fifty-one lives.

Moving along the coast road the next village encountered is Walcott. Like Bacton, this was a sleepy fishing hamlet for most of its life, most noted for its beach, which made an excellent landing place for vessels bringing in cargoes of coal and malt. In 1845 the village is recorded as being home to 172 souls, including a number of gentlemen and a High Constable in the form of Robert Atkinson. By 1890 the coastal trade was declining and just 101 people were listed in the village. The railway effectively killed off coastal trading and no other trade or industry emerged in the village to replace it. From 1900 the hamlet of Walcott faced an uncertain future. The village had received a whole section in trade directories in the nineteenth century, but by 1937 it was noted as a subsidiary section of the entry for Happisburgh, and it certainly did not stand out in any tourist guide, being too far and lacking any special attractions for excursions from Cromer or Yarmouth.

It could be said the greatest draw of Walcott was the village blacksmith in the late nineteenth century, John Gibbons, a man of 'stalwart frame and kindly, ruddy face, with ragged white beard'. His stentorian singing voice was noted for miles around. It was said of him that in the village choir he 'roars out the bass like the drum of a threshing machine'. What trade remained in Walcott came from passing custom on the coast road and a few holiday-retreat bungalows erected after the First World War. The holiday trade only really came to Walcott after the Second World War, when more people could afford their own cars and could drive to the village and stay in one of the growing number of timber-framed bungalows which were being erected around the village on the cliff top.

Walcott had suffered many incursions by the sea as it bit large chunks out of the agricultural land that dared to adjoin the low cliffs near the village. In the 1860s William Cubitt of Bacton Abbey recorded his recollections of lost land in the Bacton

The road through the bungalowlands of Walcott, *c.* 1930.

and Walcott areas. In the previous thirty-five years he had seen four coal yards along with a farmhouse, barn, outbuildings and a fine bowling green succumb to coastal erosion. It was well within living memory at the end of the twentieth century for people to recall not only another coast road on the seaward side of the present one but cultivated fields beyond that. The worst encroachments took place over the winter of 1952/3 when the December storms had torn away so much land that the coastal road nearly abutted the cliff edge. Sea defences were hastily erected, and these might have sufficed had not the worst storms in living memory crashed into the coast in January 1953. All of the shops and buildings immediately near the coast road were destroyed, and the chalets and bungalows on the cliff edge were smashed to firewood. A new sea wall, coast road, post office, shops and bungalows were all rebuilt afterwards – albeit a few hundred yards further inland.

Happisburgh is a fascinating and historical village, which has fought a constant battle with the sea throughout its existence. The warnings from history are found in the nearby handful of houses known as Whimpwell Green, the only remnant, and this in name only, of the fishing village of Whimpwell that stood on the seaward side of Happisburgh. Mentioned in a document dating from the reign of Henry II, this village was completely washed away during the Middle Ages. The only remaining vestige of Whimpwell is an area of masonry from some large stone building, probably the village church, which can just be discerned through the waters a short distance out to sea on particularly low tides.

The impending danger to Happisburgh was seen as so extreme that some writers in the nineteenth century were convinced that the rate of coastal erosion would

The Gap, Happisburgh. Here thousands of visitors would walk and even the lifeboat would be pulled along it to the beach. Despite concrete defences and wooden breakwaters this has now been eroded by the sea and only a fractured stump of road exists today.

Happisburgh, *c.* 1920. Most of the foreground in this photograph has since been eroded by the sea, which is now just a few hundred yards from the rear of Hill House pub.

mean the village disappearing beneath the waves within 100 years. William White expressed his view in his *Norfolk Directory* of 1845: 'The Church [St Mary] is a lofty pile, with a fine embattled tower, 112 feet high, standing on an elevated point of land, within a short distance of the sea-cliff, which, rising perpendicularly, and having an under stratum of sand and gravel, is so continually wasted by the agitation of tides and storms, that it is calculated the church will be engulfed in the ocean before the close of the ensuing century, the sea having encroached upwards of 170 yards during the last 60 years.' The same year that White's *Directory* was published it was recorded that 'a field of 12 acres on a farm called the Point because it jutted into the sea was drilled with wheat, during the night a gale from the north-west began. In the morning the whole field had disappeared.' The rate of sea erosion was well evinced by the sale deeds for what became Lighthouse Farm: when it was offered for sale in 1790 it comprised 280 acres; when it was sold in 1852 it had dwindled to just 176 acres.

At Happisburgh the toll of the sea is not just the erosion of the village and its surrounding farmland: in the churchyard may be found the mute testimony on headstones and memorials of numerous shipwrecks and bodies washed ashore on the tide. Vivid accounts of great storms casting wrecks upon the beach can be traced back to the earliest records of the village, where lords of the manor made sure they asserted their claim to the rights over the contents of wrecked ships. Records from the late eighteenth and early nineteenth centuries list many examples of such tragedies on the waters off Happisburgh, such as HMS *Peggy*, an eight-gun naval sloop which had been patrolling the waters for smugglers. Caught in the maelstrom of the great storm of 19 December 1770, which also tore down Happisburgh's old windmill, *Peggy* was dashed ashore by the Town Gap with the loss of thirty-two hands.

Village on the brink? The indefatigable beat of the waves and the eroded cliffs at Happisburgh, 2006.

Probably the greatest single tragedy off Happisburgh was the wrecking on 16 March 1801 of HMS *Invincible*, a third-rate, 74-gun, man-of-war. She had sailed up from Chatham and had put in to Yarmouth to collect orders before setting out to join the Baltic Fleet before the Battle of Copenhagen, where Norfolk's own Admiral Nelson was again to distinguish himself. HMS *Invincible* left Yarmouth carrying not only its young Captain, John Rennie, aged 34, but also Thomas Totty, Rear Admiral of the Blue. It goes without saying that *Invincible* was loaded to the gunwales with all the ordnance, food and provisions necessary for her crew of 600. A strong tide and keen wind sent the ship off course and she struck a sandbank known as Hammond's Knoll, just east of Haisbro' Sands at 2.30 p.m. Despite jettisoning some of its cargo and having hopes of rescue raised after the revenue cutter *Hunter* answered the distress signal, no assistance arrived until Yarmouth cod smack *The Nancy* came to her aid. *Invincible* was beyond rescue by midnight. An orderly evacuation was organised for the Rear Admiral and some of the youngest members of the crew. The main body of the crew waited for daybreak to be rescued, but as the sky began to brighten with the first light of dawn HMS *Invincible* went down with the loss of 400 hands; 119 members of the ship's company were buried in Happisburgh churchyard. A fine memorial was eventually erected to their memory in 1998.

It is somewhat ironic to note that the revenue cutter *Hunter* that had answered *Invincible*'s distress signal but had failed to send help came to grief herself on 18 February 1807 when she foundered just north of Cart Gap with the loss of all hands. Those whose bodies were washed ashore were buried in Happisburgh churchyard. The *Hunter* was replaced by the *Ranger*, which would become known as one of the most famous (or infamous) revenue boats of the Norfolk coast, responsible for many a seizure of 'baccy, tea and liquor'. No doubt the crew saw many of those they caught sent to the gallows. It would be truthful to say, as we have seen with many other villages along this coastline, that smuggling was a way of life for many in the area, and the revenue men were widely hated. When *Ranger* was caught in a great gale on 13 October 1822 and tossed inexorably towards the same shoals that had claimed *Hunter* fifteen years earlier, she too was lost with all hands. Rumour soon spread that the screams and distress signals of the ship had been heard by the people of Happisburgh and that 'by the shameful neglect of the inhabitants of Happisburgh neither boat nor Captain Manby's apparatus was got to the spot'.

The Ghost of the Happisburgh Smuggler

The story of the Happisburgh Smuggler is a ghostly tale that has thrilled and chilled visitors to the village for over 200 years. The ghostly, glowing apparition of a man in seaman's garb was observed at several locations and on several occasions between Cart Gap and Well Corner (Pump Hill). Upon closer observance the spectre was noted to carry a bundle and be missing his legs and, some thought, his head, but those who saw the apparition from behind saw the head had in fact been subject to a botched hacking: it was still attached by a thin strip of skin to the neck and was hanging down the phantom's back like some hideous sack, its pigtail now nearly dragging along the floor. The ghost was seen to terminate its journey at the well, where it dropped its bundle therein and then disappeared down the well himself.

On one occasion the ghost was seen by a group of farm workers, who were disbelieved when they related their tale the following day. So they decided to investigate, and a volunteer, a butcher's lad named Harmer, was sent down the 40ft or so of the well with a long clothes prop. Sure enough, he found something, and an iron hake (pot hook) tied to a clothes line was lowered down to him. The sodden object was soon hooked and hauled up. Eagerly opened by those at the well head, it revealed a pair of seaman's thigh boots – with the legs still inside! The boy Harmer had clearly been shaken by the experience, so a fisherman – filled with plenty of Dutch courage – was lowered down the well to investigate further. Another bundle was recovered and therein was the body of the unfortunate sailor, his wounds corresponding exactly with the spectre seen by the locals. Investigation of the smugglers' hideout at Cart Gap still showed signs of a mortal struggle, and a pistol that matched one found on the body was discovered at the scene. For some reason the smugglers had disagreed, perhaps over the division of spoils, or perhaps someone had opened their mouth to the wrong person or turned informer. Who the smuggler was or who had killed him was never revealed, but the well itself was capped with a pump and provided water for many generations afterwards. And on dark winter nights it is still said you may just see a glowing form between Cart Gap and Pump Hill – perhaps the Happisburgh Smuggler is still hunting for his killers!

The old lifeboat house and beach company hut, Happisburgh, *c.* 1920. After the closure of the lifeboat station both these historic structures fell into disrepair over the ensuing years and were eventually demolished.

However, the people of Happisburgh were not totally without conscience and had sought to provide at least some landmark that could be observed from the sea. Atop the lofty church tower a great wooden cross was erected, though this was badly decayed by 1818, when it was blown down in a gale. Another was soon put in its place, but as a contemporary account from 1822 states, it 'served as a conductor for the electric fluid' when struck by lightning. The cross turned into a flaming mass and collapsed, sending a great piece of masonry crashing, followed by burning fragments, through the roof of the church into the aisle below. The church caught fire and only by the swift action of villagers was the ancient building saved. It is hardly surprising that the cross was not replaced again; in any case, by that time there were other far more effective warning methods for mariners in the village.

In 1791 two lights were established in Happisburgh by the Trinity Brethren. The principal tower stood 100ft tall and another of some 80ft was positioned lower down the cliff – they soon became known as the 'High Light' and the 'Low Light'. Both were surmounted by 20ft-high lanterns lit originally by braziers fuelled, somewhat ironically, by tarry wreck wood and, later, candles. In the early nineteenth century Argand oil lamps with reflectors replaced the candles. The new reflector was heralded as a triumph at the Great Exhibition of 1851, and a report in the *Norfolk Chronicle* was effusive: 'The new apparatus for Haisborough (*sic*) resembles a huge crystal beehive which, in the sunlight, flashes with the radiance of gems – a perfect rainbow of colour.' Then in about 1865 the lights' fuel source was changed to gas produced in the vicinity of the 'High Light' in five coal-fired retorts, which was then stored nearby in two large gasholders.

On 6 August 1866 Happisburgh received its first lifeboat from the RNLI – the 32ft, ten-oared self-righting type *Huddersfield*, with its boatshed at Old Cart Gap. Beside this new 'substantial and commodious' lifeboat house was the beachmen's shed, complete with its unique decor of washed-up name boards and sea-worn figurehead beside it. The lifeboat was launched by a team of horses, which would pull the craft on its carriage across the beach and into the water. For the first twenty-three years the horses used for every drill and service launch were supplied by Mr William Wilkins. When he died in 1890 a gratuity of £5 was granted to his widow in recognition of his services. In its forty years at Happisburgh *Huddersfield* saved fifty-one lives.

The two lights of Happisburgh beamed out together until 1883, when concern was aroused about the deterioration of the cliffs and the 'High Light' was converted from a fixed beacon to an occulting light. Soon after that it received the first painting of its distinctive red and white stripes, and a new light vessel was established out to sea. The old 'Low Light' was sold by tender and demolished soon afterwards. Happisburgh's lifeboat was replaced in 1887 by a new boat, also named *Huddersfield*. However, she was soon considered inadequate: the lifeboatmen wanted a boat with a greater beam that would give it a better range and enable the offshore sandbanks to be reached. The next and final boat to serve this station, *Jacob and Rachel Valentine*, arrived in November 1907. She had been sent by the M&GN Railway to Stalham and was then conveyed by road to the lifeboat station.

If the intentions of the local railway companies had been brought to fruition the Happisburgh lifeboat could have got all the way to the village by train. In the late nineteenth century the GER proposed schemes for an extension of the line from Mundesley to Happisburgh with a further extension southwards to Sea Palling, Horsey and Great Yarmouth in 1896. The proposal got as far as an Act of Parliament for the connection of Knapton by a junction with the authorised branch of the Midland & Great Northern Joint Railway, terminating in the parish of Happisburgh. A terrace of railway houses was built and a signal box was even erected at the rear of Hill House in 1901. At Stalham station there was a grand sign announcing the new connections: 'Stalham for Happisburgh & Palling on Sea'. But even the railway could see that neither the dream of Poppyland nor the overspill of Yarmouth could stretch this far. They could see Mundesley was not experiencing the boom they had envisaged when they built their grand multi-platform station there. The Happisburgh line was not to be and the scheme was abandoned in 1902, leaving the signal box and railway terrace as enigmatic reminders of the railway that never was.

The next three decades were to see the end of an era for the Happisburgh lights and lifeboats. The *Jacob and Rachel Valentine*, which was always launched by a team of ten horses from Love's Farm, served Happisburgh until 1926, launching on service sixteen times and saving nineteen lives. In 1926 the RNLI decided the function of the Happisburgh boat could be covered by Cromer and closed the station. In 1910 the lighthouse had been converted to an incandescent oil burner, and in 1936 it was finally converted to electricity. By this time the Happisburgh light was an unwatched beacon and the adjoining keepers' cottages had been sold. It may

Bringing in the Happisburgh lifeboat *Jacob and Rachel Valentine, c.* 1909.

have looked as if the great traditions were coming to an end, especially by 1955 when the old lifeboat shed had become so neglected that it was demolished. Ten years later the RNLI stationed an inshore rescue boat at Happisburgh. A new boathouse was built (replaced by a newer, enlarged building in 1988), and the great work of voluntary lifesaving continues to this day. In 1987 the future of the lighthouse came under threat when Trinity House gave notice of closure. The grand old light was only narrowly saved by a team of locals led by Kay Swann, who formed the Happisburgh Lighthouse Trust and gained a private Act of Parliament and Royal Assent to save it. With any luck, the light's future, with a 99-year lease, is now secure in their hands.

A couple of miles along the beach from Happisburgh stood the town of Eccles. Today this is a mere scattering of houses, but before the constant encroachments of the sea it was a considerable fishing town said to have covered some 2,000 acres; above all others, if people talk of the lost villages of Norfolk the name of Eccles comes to the fore. Eccles was noted in the Domesday survey and can easily be seen from early records to be a flourishing fishing town comparable with another lost Norfolk town, Shipden. In 1305 William le Parker was Lord of the Manor with legal rights 'to all wreck at sea, toll, lagan and resting geld' as well as a 'free warren, free bull and boar, weyf and stray', the right to felons, goods and the 'liberty of gallows' to mete out his own justice. There was even a toll on every fishing boat that washed its nets within the village boundaries; between Michaelmas (29 September) and Martlemas (11 November or Martinmas) boats were even charged an additional 100 herrings for the privilege – the fishing must have been good here!

Poor Eccles was never a stranger to sea outrages. Flooding was frequent, cottages were regularly moved further inland, and the first parish church was claimed by the sea before a new one was erected in the 1330s. The situation declined by the sixteenth century to the extent that local gent William Laurod was so convinced of the town's watery fate that he specifically requested in his will of 1597 that he be buried in the neighbouring churchyard at Hempstead.

The final straw for the town of Eccles came in the teeth of the violent storm of 4 January 1604. In this one night the sea consumed the entire settlement. The sea defences were breached and 2,000 acres of marsh, wood and arable land were inundated by sea water. Sixty-six houses and most of their occupants were swept away, and the main body of the parish church was destroyed, leaving the disembodied tower like a silent sentinel standing over the scene of devastation. In 1605 the remaining residents of Eccles sent a plea to the Norwich Quarter Sessions for an easing of taxes, because only 300 acres and 14 householders out of the former 1,400 acres and 80 householders were left after the storm. Over the ensuing years sea encroachments have gradually and completely overtaken the medieval village. In the early nineteenth century the church tower was on the landward side of the marrams, by 1850 it was in the centre of the sand hills, and after the severe winter storms of 1862 it was on the beachside. Sea scours have occasionally revealed parts of the ancient village. Local coastguard Captain King RN noted in his log on 27 December 1862, 'To the north of the church considerable remains of cottages are laid bare, the very roads and ditches are visible.' Closer inspection revealed

Eccles church and beach looking toward Happisburgh, from Hewitt's *Essay on the Encroachments of the German Ocean along the Norfolk Coast*, 1844.

Beside the 'Garden of Sleep' this embattled tower of Eccles church is one of the most poignant reminders of what has been lost from the Norfolk coast. Photographed in about 1890, the tower finally succumbed to the waves in January 1895.

Over the years a number of sea scours have revealed the remnants of the lost village of Eccles. These remains of the church were revealed in about 1916.

The church and great barn, Waxham, *c.* 1935.

20 acres of previously submerged woodland along with a road leading to the ancient town upon which even the old ruts caused by cartwheels and the impressions of horseshoes could be discerned. Ernest Suffling visited the site after a scour in the winter of 1880/1 and recorded his experience in *Land of the Broads* (1895): '[I] was surprised to see the overthrown walls of the church exposed to view and also the foundations of the cottages which once formed the village. There were to be seen the decayed wooden thresholds of cottage doors, circular wells and other signs of a buried village. Close to the church walls several graves were washed open, and the bones floated about the beach by the tide.'

A curious custom was observed in the remnants of the church until it finally disappeared: a sermon was preached there at least once a year, for which the sinecure rector would receive a rent charge of £54. The tower drew many visitors and was a feature eagerly anticipated by the passengers on the thrice-weekly pleasure-steamer trips between Yarmouth and Cromer in the 1880s. The tower was finally brought down by the sea on 23 January 1895. Stalwart visitor Ernest Suffling had been walking on the beach on the 22nd and stood in the shelter of the tower to obtain a light for his pipe before retiring homeward as the tide was coming in. The 23rd broke out stormy and no one could get near the tower because of the high seas. Suffling noted, 'As the tide rose the tower received the full force of both sea and gale. I watched the great waves breaking in thunder and bombarding the tower with timber, piles and planks from demolished breakwaters. . . . Between 6 and 7 o'clock the tower fell but no-one saw its fall. . . . On the 24th many persons came to see the fallen patriarch, and each, with myself, agreed that it seemed like standing beside a dead friend.'

This tractor and reaper, which were completely submerged during the Horsey floods in February 1938, started up when the magneto and points were dried off.

The coastline between Eccles and Winterton has also been subject to regular, dramatic incursions by the sea. As early as December 1287 a great 'rage of the sea' breached the coastline and swept across the land to Hickling, drowning 180 in its wake. At Waxham only one wing remains of the once-grand Mockbeggar's Hall, originally built in the early twelfth century when it was said to be 12 miles inland. Today the sea laps little more than 200yd from its gatehouse. At nearby Horsey the River Thurne (the old Hundred Stream) joined the sea. Known to the Romans this waterway gradually silted up and sandhills replaced its estuary. During severe storms of the last 500 years the sea appears to have done its best to reinstate the old water channel. Encroachments of recent centuries include those of 1607, 1611, 1665, 1741, 1791 and 1897, but the floods remembered by most locals here happened on the night of 13 February 1938. The sea had been whipped into a frenzy by a northerly gale, and damage was caused at several locations along the east coast. But it was here at Horsey, which is only 8ft 11in above sea level, and on the nearby Broads that disaster occurred when a tidal wave smashed through the sea defences causing a 700yd breach, the biggest for fifty years. A 9ft-tall wall of water thundered across the marshes, and sea and broad merged as one. Horsey village was inundated and a total area of 15 square miles of neighbouring villages, farms and marshes was flooded. Several villages were evacuated; it is amazing that nobody was killed by the flood, though many livestock were lost. The East Norfolk River Catchment Board assessed the damage at the time to be about £13,000 in Horsey alone. It took months for the rust-brown sludge and tidelines on properties and countryside to fade or be removed, and years rather than months for the farmland to recover its viability for cultivation.

The most severe damage and loss to this section of the coast in modern times occurred at Sea Palling during the night of Saturday 31 January/Sunday 1 February 1953. Before the flood Beach Road in Palling was a typical Norfolk seaside destination, with a blend of flint-faced private homes, a restaurant and cafe for tourists, and the affectionately remembered Lifeboat Inn. When the tidal wave hit in the midst of some of the highest winds on record local people stood little chance of survival. Numerous properties were simply washed away or smashed beyond repair. Seven people died. When the waters receded sand covered Beach Road, lying in drifts up to 5ft deep. Although buildings were built anew and a massive sea-defence wall was undertaken, Sea Palling would never be quite the same again, and the innocence of this quiet seaside village was lost forever.

We complete our journey along this section of the coast at Winterton. If the sea claims its land toll most ruthlessly at Happisburgh and Eccles, its toll of shipping is claimed most severely at Winterton. Today Winterton Ness has been scoured away by the sea to appear as little more than a slight bump on an ordnance survey map, but more ancient cartography, such as Christopher Saxton's map of Norfolk of 1574, shows Winterton Ness as a clear promontory jutting out beyond the village and out to sea to the extent of over 1¾ miles. Here a small, seasonal fishing township was established from early medieval times. The sea waters around here were the most dangerous of the series of sandbanks that fringe the coast from Cromer down to Haisbro', sands known collectively as the Devil's Throat; here at Winterton Ness, the

Beach Road, Sea Palling, *c.* 1931.

The view across the Beach Road area at Sea Palling in the aftermath of the east-coast flood disaster of 1953.

The sturdy sea defences erected and maintained by various schemes at Sea Palling since the east-coast floods in 1953.

The Fisherman's Return pub, Winterton, *c*. 1910.

sandbank was known to mariners as the most fatal headland between Scotland and London. Winterton Ness has a long history of horrendous shipwrecks; they include such incidents as that of 1554 when over fifty ships were wrecked on the Ness during a single stormy day. In 1692 a fleet of 200 sail of colliers had just left the waters of the 'Yarmouth Roads' in a fair wind when they were assailed by a violent nor'easterly gale. One hundred and forty sail were 'driven ashore, completely wrecked', and scarcely any of their crews were saved. Many was the local store which became stacked high with the cargoes washed up and salvaged from the shore; local people were far from wasteful, and many used washed-up ships' timbers in the construction of their houses and outbuildings. Indeed, as Daniel Defoe observed of Winterton in 1722, 'There was not a shed, nor a barn, nor a stable, nay not the pales of their fences and yards, not a hogstye but what was made of planks, beams, whales and timbers, the wreck of ships and the ruin of merchants' and mariners' fortunes.'

With such a history of shipwrecks it is hardly surprising that Winterton had one of the earliest, and certainly most dominant, companies of Norfolk beachmen. By the early nineteenth century there were two companies of beachmen in Winterton. The 'Young 'Uns' (mostly Methodists) were based in their shed or 'court' in the sand hills along with their tall wooden lookout to the north of the parish gap; the longer-established 'Old 'Uns' shed, built on the southern side of the gap, was disparagingly known as 'Hell's Kitchen'.

The two Winterton Beach Companies did not get on until the Palling Beach Company was founded and began to encroach on the 'turf', or rather the 'sea space', of the Winterton men. Soon the old quarrels between the Winterton men

The Old Un's beachmen's lookout and headquarters, Winterton, *c.* 1905.

were forgotten, and they formed a united front of abuse and common dislike of 'Pallingers'. The primary concern for the companies of beachmen was earning salvage money, and plenty there was to be made too. Beach companies could be awarded hundreds of pounds for salvage by Admiralty courts. Sums such as an award of 100 guineas for the gun brig *Mastiff* in 1800 or £276 5*s* for the schooner *Ney Prove* of Copenhagen in 1810 were quite typical. There was always a race to get to ships in danger. Young and Old companies would dash to their sheds to drag their boats to water; both wanted to get there first and both certainly wanted to arrive before the 'Pallingers'. Handsome amounts could also be negotiated with stranded captains when the beachmen were accepted on board stricken vessels. Terms would have to be formally agreed between the rescue boat coxswain and the ship's captain and mediated by the beach company 'sea lawyer' (usually the most loquacious of the beachmen) before any rescue was undertaken!

This said, the beachmen were not so merciless as to let men die if they could help it. Many brave rescues were carried out by the beachmen, although it has to be said that in the backs of their minds there was always hope of a financial reward for lifesaving – such as the grant of 25 guineas given to Abel King and William Pile for special bravery in the *Mastiff* rescue. In 1857 the lifeboat station at Winterton was taken over by the RNLI, and the first boat *Ann Maria* was sent to the station the following year. A No. 2 station was established in 1870, and it is hardly surprising that the beachmen made up the crews. It is also worthy of note that the seamanship of born-and-bred Winterton men was renowned in the area, even as far down as Great Yarmouth, where they skippered the majority of fishing boats out of the port. With old rivalries put aside by the 1860s, Winterton men provided coxswains for lifeboats at Palling, Winterton, California, Caister, Yarmouth and on one of the Gorleston boats.

A lighthouse was established by the Trinity Bretheren at Winterton in the early years of the seventeenth century. They did not have a patent and thus could not demand dues as a legal right. To overcome the problem they instigated a voluntary toll of 6*d* per chaldron (25cwt) of coals carried on trading vessels. Ship owners appeared to have been happy to pay this toll for the maintenance of a beacon to warn of the fateful Winterton Ness. James I did, however, grant a patent to Sir John Meldrum for a lighthouse, and the Trinity Bretheren were ordered to remove their voluntary light. Meldrum constructed a pair of lights at Winterton with another pair out on the Ness, and so passing mariners were given some warning of these dangerous waters for the next 200 years. In 1830 Winterton Ness had become so depleted it was decided not to maintain the lights upon it, and the two towers were demolished. The remaining stations at Winterton were purchased by Trinity House in 1837. The old structures were demolished and the lighthouse that still stands today was erected in their stead. The new lighthouse stood 70ft high, and in 1840 'two neat houses were erected on the cliff' for the lighthousemen. In 1843 a floating light was placed in the 'Cockle Gatt' at the north entrance to the Yarmouth Roads. This was fitted 'with a first-class dioptric light' in 1867. In the 1870s Winterton light was subject to another rebuild and it was painted all red to contrast with the Happisburgh lights' red and white stripes. At night the lights could be told apart because Happisburgh blinked its occulting light, giving an eclipse of five seconds each half-minute, and Winterton shone a fixed light. By the end of the

The crew and Winterton No. 2 lifeboat, *Eleanor Brown*, which served between 1909 until the station closed and the boat was withdrawn by the RNLI in 1925.

Winterton lighthouse, *c.* 1909.

First World War there were so many lights and buoys out to sea that the Winterton light was considered superfluous. Mr Squibb, the last full-time lighthouse keeper, retired, and the old lighthouse was auctioned off at the Star Hotel, Great Yarmouth for £1,550. Today all that remains is the decapitated tower, which has become part of the surrounding holiday park.

With cover provided by fast, motorised vessels from Cromer, Caister, Yarmouth and Gorleston, the main lifeboat station was closed by the RNLI in 1925. The lifeboat sheds fell into disrepair and were taken down. An interesting observation made at the demolition was that when the lifeboat houses were new their ramps led down to the water's edge, whereas when demolished they were 250yd inland from it, and 150yd inland from the dunes! In fact a new coastguard watch-house had to be erected in 1960 because by then the old one was too far away from the water to have a commanding view. Unlike so many of its coastal counterparts Winterton has a firmly established ridge of dunes which gains land through the tides rather than having it washed away. Perhaps we have not heard the last of Winterton Ness.

CHAPTER 7

Great Yarmouth – Red Herrings and Happy Holidays

''Twas raised from the waters and built on the bones of herring.'
(Old saying about Great Yarmouth)

In the concluding chapter of this book it will be demonstrated that the sea not only erodes away land and settlements but also can create spits of land for new ones. The best example of this in Norfolk is Great Yarmouth. The Norfolk known to its Roman invaders did not include Great Yarmouth. At that time the entire area now occupied by the town was a broad estuary where three great rivers joined together and emptied into the sea. The area where Halvergate Marshes now stand was tidal mudflats, and the districts of Flegg and Lothingland were islands. The width of this great tract of water can be easily measured when we consider the foreshore forts that commanded safe anchorages to the north and south of the estuary mouth: one at Burgh Castle, the other at Caister. Towards the end of the Roman period sea levels fell all around Britain and a sandbank emerged where Great Yarmouth now stands. The shallow waters around this area were excellent feeding grounds for herring, and very soon a seasonal settlement was established there by the fishermen who followed the shoals of herring down the east coast. These fishermen's huts gradually grew into the permanent town of Great Yarmouth. Victorian and Edwardian commentators remarked, having seen the vast herring trade conducted in those days and the affluence it brought, that Yarmouth was a town built on herring. They probably did not realise how accurate they were: recent archaeological bores sunk around Great Yarmouth have all revealed deep in the geological strata layers of herring bones from the medieval fishing trade.

By the mid-fourteenth century the mouth of the River Yare was silting up, and threatened the shipping navigation to the quayside. Early attempts to dig out a haven were problematic and often abortive; no doubt Yarmouth feared the same fate as that which befell the Glaven Ports, where the sandbanks eventually meant only the smallest ships could reach the quays and others had to be winched across the sands to enter the harbour. It was only in 1567 when the Dutch engineer Joas

The Quay, Great Yarmouth, 1855.

Johnson was employed that an effective solution was found. Having encountered and dealt with similar problems in Holland he set about directing works to erect two stone and timber piers to contain the river. The entire works on this haven were completed in 1614 and cost the town dearly. In 1567, to defray some of the costs, the town invested heavily in the first state lottery, and in 1614 in the Virginia state lottery – they won neither. Although the costs remained a burden the sea channel was kept clear; trade was restored and this seventh haven is still in use today.

The early town of Yarmouth was constructed along a grid pattern whereby the settlers were allotted a strip of land with a section of foreshore and some higher ground upon which their houses were built. There were narrow lanes between these strips to enable access between the river and the beach. As the population grew these strips were divided into housing plots with the rights of way retained, which became the passageways of the 'Rows'. There were over 145 of these distinctive lines of terraced, cheek-by-jowl houses and cottages, where the ordinary people of Yarmouth lived until bombing during the Second World War and housing improvements of the postwar years saw the majority of the Rows demolished and their way of life lost forever.

Yarmouth was first and foremost a fishing port. By the thirteenth century herring had become one of the staple foods of England, and Yarmouth was the fifth-wealthiest town in the country. Although the clamour for herring fluctuated from

A typical Great Yarmouth Row, *c.* 1905.

The central beach, Great Yarmouth, in its heyday in the 1890s.

time to time, the trade continued and Yarmouth sent herrings all over Britain, Europe and beyond for another 600 years. Daniel Defoe recorded after his visit in 1722 that local merchants claimed to have cured 40,000 barrels of herring a season, but the greatest expansion of the Yarmouth herring industry came during the nineteenth century. The fishing boats were improved, and new ones were built with innovations that enabled them to haul up unprecedented catches. The Yarmouth herring industry depended on export trade, and fish were preserved through smoking or curing, so that by 1850 more than sixty curing houses operated in the town. The coming of the railways enabled faster and more efficient distribution, and the construction of the new fish wharf in 1869 meant better landing and selling facilities for the catches. The improved fishing boats or 'drifters' began fishing further afield, going north in the summer and returning to their home fishery. In the winter they would go south or change their rig and go trawling in the North Sea.

Sea trade and fishing have also prompted many of the towns and villages we have encountered in this book to set up rescue measures such as beach companies and lifeboats. Yarmouth was no exception; beach companies were established with tall wooden lookout towers, yawls and headquarters dotted along the seafront from the eighteenth century onwards, and probably years earlier. By 1860 there were no fewer than seven companies of beachmen in the town, by far the greatest concentration at any one point along the coast. The town was also home to one of the greatest innovators of lifesaving devices, Captain George Manby, who was Master of the Great Yarmouth Artillery in the early nineteenth century. Among his inventions was a line-throwing mortar, the precursor of the modern rocket apparatus used to rescue crews from shipwrecked vessels. His device was tested on Yarmouth Beach in July 1807 and proved highly effective. Approved by the Admiralty in January 1808, it was first successfully employed the following month in saving the crew of *Elizabeth of Plymouth*, and was soon adopted at rescue stations all around the coast. In 1823 the Norfolk Shipwreck Association had Yarmouth's first purpose-built lifeboat (also designed by Manby) installed on the beach. In 1858 the Shipwrecked Sailors' Home was also built. This institution closed in 1964 and the building became home to the Maritime Museum; today it houses the Great Yarmouth Tourist Office. In 1859 the RNLI took over from the Norfolk Shipwreck Association and erected a lifeboat station. Yarmouth's last boat, the *Hugh Taylor*, served from 1912 to 1919, when the station was closed and its responsibilities were passed to the Gorleston lifeboat. Until recently there were still those who remembered with affection how they would help land the old Yarmouth boat out of its boathouse by manhandled ropes across Marine Parade and down the beach to the sea for services and practice drills.

As the fishing boats followed the herring shoals so did the Scots; the men on the boats, the women by road or steamer and later by train, because women were considered unlucky on fishing boats. The Scots brought more innovation and efficiency to the herring industry, including machine-made cotton nets in the 1860s. After the development of the steam-powered drifter in the 1880s and the resultant increased catching power, the Scots led the way in developing new markets for brine-cured herring in Germany and Russia, a market which was to eventually overtake the traditional trade in smoked red herring. By the mid-1880s there were generally more Scottish than home boats fishing from Yarmouth each autumn. The

The wreck of the *Anna Precht* on Yarmouth Beach after the gales, 18 September 1906.

The crew of the Great Yarmouth lifeboat *John Burch* wearing their oilskins, sou'westers and cork life jackets, *c.* 1905.

Some of the Scottish fisher girls packing herring in barrels, Great Yarmouth, *c.* 1920.

The air is thick with smoke from the funnels of the returning fishing fleet as they pass by the lighthouse on Gorleston Harbour, *c.* 1920.

Scottish fisher girls came down by the thousand to gut, salt and pickle herring in the vast curing yards that spread across the South Denes. These girls became one of the sights of Yarmouth. When gutting their hands were a blur, the sharp knives they used seen as an occasional flash when the wet blade caught the sun. One girl was timed as gutting fifty-seven fish in a minute. Even when not at work the girls made quite a sight as they walked broadside on in lines about the town, gossiping furiously in a Scottish brogue barely intelligible to the locals. As they walked and talked they knitted to keep their fingers nimble, rarely looking at their work; using this sense of touch they seldom dropped a stitch.

By 1907 it was estimated that visiting Scottish workers, including fishermen, coopers, fisher girls and curers, swelled the town's population by about 10,000 in the season. In 1913 about 1,000 vessels fished from Yarmouth; when they docked to unload, the smoke from the funnels of the steamers filled the air like a smog, and it was said you could walk across the lined-up bows of ships from Yarmouth to Gorleston. The year 1913 was the heyday of the Yarmouth herring trade. In the three-month season of that year 824,213 cran (a cran was 1,132 herring and weighed about 28 stone), worth nearly £1 million, were landed at Yarmouth.

The First World War brought an abrupt halt to the herring trade when many drifters were taken into the service of the Admiralty as minesweepers; many of their crews bravely joined this service too. After revolution in Russia and the loss

Landing herrings at the Fish Wharf, Great Yarmouth, late 1940s.

of German markets the main trade outlets dried up, and although there were still markets in Africa, India and across the Mediterranean, the first nail had already been knocked into the coffin of the herring industry. After the war, it has to be admitted, there was a boom in demand and everyone looked forward to the return of the herring heyday; but great gluts of fish one year were followed by dearths the next. In the Second World War the drifters and crews were called up again and used by the Royal Naval Patrol Service in the same role of minesweeping. The trade was again disrupted, so that when the war ended in 1945 the foreign markets had all but dried up and owners were driven to sell their vessels as debts rose. Those fishing boats that were left had to become efficient and technically advanced. Furthermore, the herring stocks became depleted and overfishing damaged the grounds that served as nurseries for immature fish. After 1953 catches declined every year. In 1966 no fishing boats came at all and by the end of that decade herring fishing from Great Yarmouth had ceased altogether.

Yarmouth was, however, fortunate because it had two sources of prosperity. The harbour and fishery were on the landward of the original sand spar, while on the seaward was the sea and a sea frontage that had proved to be its second fortune. Following Dr Russell's popular theories published in 1753, the gentry took to sea bathing for medicinal purposes. In 1759 work was commenced on the Great Yarmouth Bathhouse on waste ground near the jetty purchased by Charles

The jetty and beach, Great Yarmouth, 1871.

The beach and Britannia pier, Great Yarmouth, 1871.

The Revolving Tower, seen here in about 1910, was built in 1897. Standing 120ft high, the tower had a cage capable of holding 150 people, which rotated as it went up and down to give panoramic views across Yarmouth and the sea front. One of only five such towers in the country, it was considered too much of a landmark for enemy bombers so it was demolished in 1941 and the metal sent for war salvage.

Britannia Pier, Great Yarmouth *c.* 1920.

The development of Gorleston, *c.* 1890. A small cluster of fishermen's sheds, houses and the haunt of many an old salt, the Anchor of Hope pub.

By about 1912 the scene had changed beyond recognition. The Pier Hotel, Pavilion Theatre Beach Gardens with bandstand and bustling beach show the new Gorleston seaside resort.

The heyday of Gorleston in the 1920s. Here are the new gardens which were laid out in 1924 with the grand bandstand which had been moved from Yarmouth sea front. These developments were accompanied by the construction of a model yacht pond and paddling pool in 1926. Stretching out to sea extended the old Dutch pier known as 'the cosies'. Tragically the cosies was destroyed in 1964 when the pier was rebuilt and faced with concrete.

Marine Parade, Great Yarmouth, 1930s.

de Grys. Built for the grand sum in its day of £2,000, it opened in 1760 offering 'two commodious Sea Baths, one for gentlemen, one for ladies'. The sea water was raised every tide by a horse-drawn pump mill into a reservoir about 50yd from the bathhouse, and conveyed to the bath by pipes. The nineteenth century saw the Marine Parade area popularised by gentry. Bathing machines appeared on the beach, and many fine seaward-facing hotels and terraces were built in styles similar to Brighton. In 1859 the railway came to Yarmouth, eventually bringing visitors of all classes in their thousands during the holiday season; pleasure piers were erected along with more hotels and guest houses, theatres, an aquarium, a circus, cinemas, concert-party rings, penny arcades and even, at the turn of the century, a pleasure beach with a wooden scenic railway. The adjoining village of Gorleston welcomed the overspill onto its then large beach, which soon had a 'tent village' assembled on its own sands every season, and its own pavilion theatre, guesthouses, hotel and rows of terraced houses where the sleepy fishing village had once stood. Yarmouth, the town that had risen from the waters and was built on the bones of herring, would never be the same again.

Select Bibliography

Adamson, Simon H., *Seaside Piers*, Batsford, 1977

Anckorn, Gordon, *A West Norfolk Camera*, Ashgrove, 1981

Arnott, Ken, *Hunstanton*, Borough Council of King's Lynn, 2000

Ashwin, Trevor and Davison, Alan (eds), *An Historical Atlas of Norfolk*, Phillimore, 2005

Belton, Valerie, *The Norwich to Cromer Turnpike*, Belton, 1998

Birch, Mel, *Historic East Anglia in Camera*, Images Publications, 1988

Blake, P.W., *The Norfolk We Live In* (rev. edn), Jarrold, 1964

Bond, Richard, Penn, Kenneth and Rogerson, Andrew, *The North Folk: Angles, Saxons and Danes*, Poppyland, 1990

Brooks, Peter, *Sheringham: The Story of a Town*, Poppyland, 1980

——, *Have You Hears About Blakeney?*, Poppyland, 1981

——, *Cley: Living With Memories of Greatness*, Poppyland, 1984

——, *Salthouse: Village of Character and History*, Poppyland, 1984

Clark, Ronald H., *A Short History of the Midland and Great Northern Railway*, Goose, 1967

Cooke, W.H., *Eccles next the Sea and The Erosion of the East Coast*, privately published collection of notes, 1908

Cox, Peter, *The Divided Village*, Courtyard, 2000

Crawford Holden, C., *Cromer: The Cutting of the Gem*, Poppyland, 1979

Dence, Colin, *Portrait of a Village: Castle Rising*, Dence, 1980

Goodwyn, E.A., *Cromer Past*, Bidnall, *c*. 1970

——, *Mundesley Past*, Bidnall, *c*. 1970

Gurney, David, *Outposts of the Roman Empire*, Norfolk Archaeological Trust, 2002

Hedges, A.A.C., *East Coast Shipping*, Shire, 1974

——, *What to See in Great Yarmouth and District*, Weathercock, 1978

Hewitt, W., *An Essay on the Encroachments of the German Ocean Along the Norfolk Coast with a Design to Arrest its Further Depredations*, Matchett & Stevenson, 1844

Higgins, David, *The Beachmen*, Dalton, 1987

Jolly, Cyril, *Henry Blogg of Cromer*, Harrap, 1958

Knox, Margaret, *Norfolk*, Shire, 1989

Leach, Nicholas, *The Happisburgh Lifeboats*, Norfolk & Suffolk Research Group, 1999

Lewis, Charles, *Great Yarmouth History, Herrings and Holidays*, Poppyland, 1980

Linnell, C.L.S., *Blakeney Church* (rev. edn), Ashlock, 1984

Long, Neville, *The Norfolk Coast*, Dibb, 1968

Mackie, Charles, *Norfolk Annals*, Norfolk Chronicle, 1901

Malster, Bob and Stibbons, Peter, *The Cromer Lifeboats* (rev. edn), Poppyland, 1994

Mee, Arthur, *The King's England: Norfolk*, (Hodder, 1940, and (rev. edn), Hodder, 1970

Morris, Revd D., *Geography of the County of Norfolk*, Collins, 1870

Morris, John and Brown, Philippa (eds), *Domesday Book, Norfolk*, Phillimore, 1984

Pestell, Ronnie, *Happisburgh: The Story of a Coastal Parish*, Harrison, 1972

Pipe, Christopher, *The Story of Cromer Pier*, Poppyland, 1998

Reading, Eric, *A Mundesley Album*, Poppyland, 1985

Robinson, Bruce, *Norfolk Fragments*, Elmstead, 1994

—— and Gregory, Tony, *Celtic Fire and Roman Rule*, Poppyland, 1987

Sabin, Veronica, 'Bare Ruin'd Choirs: The Carmelite Friary at Burnham Norton' in *Burnham Market Records and Recollections*, Burnham Market Society, 1994

Scott, Clement, *Poppyland*, Jarrold, 1894

de Soissons, Maurice, *Brancaster Staithe: The Story of a Norfolk Fishing Village*, Woodthorpe, 1993

Steers, J.A., (ed.), *Blakeney Point and Scolt Head Island*, National Trust, 1964

Steggall, Peter, *East Anglia*, Hale, 1979

Stibbons, Peter and Cleveland, David, *Poppyland: Strands of Norfolk History*, Poppyland, 1981

——, Lee, Katherine and Warren, Martin, *Crabs and Shannocks*, Poppyland, 1983

Stibbons, Theo, *The Hunstanton Lifeboats*, Poppyland, 1984

Storey Neil R., *Norfolk at Work*, Sutton, 1997

——, *Historic Britain from the Air – Norfolk*, Sutton, 1999

——, *The North Norfolk Coast*, Sutton, 2001

——, *Flood Alert – Norfolk*, Sutton, 2003

——, *The Norfolk Coast*, Frith, 2005

Suffling, Ernest, *The Land of the Broads*, Perry, 1895

Tooke, Colin, *Great Yarmouth and Gorleston Beside the Sea*, Tookes Books, 2001

Warren, Martin, *Around Cromer*, Sutton, 1995

Weston, Chris and Sarah, *Claimed by the Sea*, Wood Green, 1994

Wiltshire, Roger, *Norfolk's Lifeboats*, SB Publications, 1994

Wrottesley, A.J., *The Midland & Great Northern Joint Railway*, David & Charles, 1970

Index